D0915237

crucial
conversations

crucial
conversations
— **THIRD EDITION** —

TOOLS FOR TALKING WHEN
STAKES ARE HIGH

JOSEPH GRENNY • KERRY PATTERSON • RON McMILLAN
AL SWITZLER • EMILY GREGORY

NEW YORK CHICAGO SAN FRANCISCO ATHENS LONDON
MADRID MEXICO CITY MILAN NEW DELHI
SINGAPORE SYDNEY TORONTO

5 6 7 8 9   LCR   26 25 24 23

ISBN   978-1-260-47418-3   (paperback)
MHID   1-260-47418-6   (paperback)

ISBN   978-1-260-47421-3   (hardcover)
MHID   1-260-47421-6   (hardcover)

e-ISBN   978-1-260-47419-0
e-MHID   1-260-47419-4

Library of Congress Cataloging-in-Publication Data
Names: Grenny, Joseph, author. | Patterson, Kerry, author. | McMillan, Ron, author. | Switzler, Al, author. | Gregory, Emily, author.
Title: Crucial conversations / Joseph Grenny, Kerry Patterson, Ron McMillan, Al Switzler, and Emily Gregory.
Description: 3rd edition. | New York : McGraw Hill, [2022] | Includes bibliographical references and index.
Identifiers: LCCN 2021027822 (print) | LCCN 2021027823 (ebook) | ISBN 9781260474183 (paperback) | ISBN 9781260474190 (ebook)
Subjects: LCSH: Interpersonal communication. | Interpersonal relations.
Classification: LCC BF637.C45 C78 2022 (print) | LCC BF637.C45 (ebook) | DDC 153.6—dc23
LC record available at https://lccn.loc.gov/2021027822
LC ebook record available at https://lccn.loc.gov/2021027823

McGraw Hill books are available at special quantity discounts to use as premiums and sales promotions or for use in corporate training programs. To contact a representative, please visit the Contact Us pages at www.mhprofessional.com.

We dedicate this book to Celia, Louise, Bonnie, Linda, and Alan—
whose support is abundant, whose love is nourishing,
and whose patience is just shy of infinite.

And to our children Christine, Rebecca, Taylor, Scott, Aislinn, Cara,
Seth, Samuel, Hyrum, Amber, Megan, Chase, Hayley, Bryn, Amber,
Laura, Becca, Rachael, Benjamin, Meridith, Lindsey, Kelley, Todd,
Spencer, Steven, Katelyn, Bradley, Anna, Sara, Rebecca, Maren, Tessa,
and Henry, who have been a wonderful source of learning.

And to our extended family of hundreds of colleagues, tens of
thousands of certified trainers, and millions of clients who have
shared the journey that brought these ideas to their present form.
They have been the models of what works. And to our patient
partners as we've labored through our own Crucial Conversations.
We are honored today to be part of a global community of gifted
teachers and practitioners who dedicate their lives to both living and
sharing principles that make the world work better for everyone.

CONTENTS

Contents

PART II

HOW TO OPEN YOUR MOUTH

PART III

HOW TO FINISH

PREFACE

When we first published *Crucial Conversations* in 2002, we made a bold claim. We argued that the root cause of many—if not most—human problems lies in how people behave when we disagree about high-stakes, emotional issues. We suggested that dramatic improvements in organizational performance were possible if people learned the skills routinely practiced by those who have found a way to master these high-stakes, *crucial moments.*

If anything, our conviction in this principle has grown in the subsequent decades. A growing body of research evidence shows that when leaders create a culture of intellectual and emotional honesty, nuclear power plants are safer, workplaces become more inclusive, financial services firms gain greater customer loyalty, hospitals save more lives, government organizations deliver better service, tech firms learn to function seamlessly across international boundaries, nonprofits execute better on their missions, and bigotry is stemmed.

But we'd be less than honest if we didn't admit that the most gratifying results we've experienced over the past 20 years have not come through research numbers, but through the thousands of stories told by courageous and skillful readers who have used these ideas to influence change when it mattered the most. One of the first was a woman who reunited with her estranged father after reading the book. A nurse described how she saved a patient's life by stepping up to a Crucial Conversation with a defensive doctor who was misreading the patient's symptoms. One man masterfully avoided a rift with siblings over a will that threatened to tear the family apart after their father's death. Two brothers broke through a decade of alienation that started when one acknowledged his sexual orientation. One intrepid reader even credits her Crucial Conversations training with helping save her life during a carjacking in Brazil.

Multiply these stories by our more than five million readers, and you'll have a sense of the meaning and satisfaction we've derived from our relationship with people like you.

WHAT'S NEW?

We've made a number of important changes in this new edition, which we believe will make this book an even more powerful resource. Some of the changes demonstrate how concepts apply to modern modes of communication. These days many of our most Crucial Conversations happen via video, asynchronous social media, audio, or, heaven forbid, text-only modes of communication. We've learned a great deal about what works and what doesn't in these domains. We've done a great deal of work in the past decade studying what it takes to surface and confront issues of diversity, inclusion, and even unconscious bias. One of our landmark studies involved over 13,000 subjects to test the effects of some of the skills we can now share. Other changes address new ways of working and new stresses that result from our increasingly global and heterogenous society. Crucial Conversations take on heightened importance as remote relationships and diverse cultures are now the norm rather than a novel exception in most workplaces. Finally, in recent years we've seen increasing evidence that dangerous conflict results from the failure to find ways to candidly and respectfully discuss our political and social differences. Some of the updates in this book will address head-on how we can all do our best when it matters most in these novel challenges.

One of the most useful changes you will notice is the restructuring of all the content in the book around an easy-to-understand model for preparing for, beginning, and concluding a Crucial Conversation. We have found that laying the skills out temporally makes it far easier for readers to know which skill to use when to get the best results.

Finally, one of the most obvious changes longtime readers will note is the addition of a new author on this edition. Emily Gregory has been an important contributor to our work for almost 20 years. She has worked shoulder to shoulder with us in deepening our research, strengthening our courses, and expanding our influence to include close to 20,000 trainers worldwide. The addition of her voice in this edition has enriched every chapter.

We are confident that not only will these changes improve your reading experience; they will also increase your capacity to turn the printed word into productive habits in your work and personal life.

WHERE NEXT?

We're thrilled that so many people have responded positively to this work. To be honest, 20 years ago we dared to hope the ideas we shared would alter the world. But what we didn't know was whether the world would respond as we hoped.

So far so good. It has been immensely gratifying to see so many people embrace the notion that Crucial Conversations really can make a difference. We've been privileged to teach heads of government, business moguls, and influential social entrepreneurs. The day we held in our hands two copies of our book—one in Arabic and one in Hebrew—gave us an even greater sense of possibility. We've shared the principles in areas of turmoil and unrest, such as Kabul and Cairo, as well as in areas of growth and influence, such as Bangkok and Benin City. With each new audience and each new success story, we feel a greater motivation to ensure our work makes a lasting difference.

Thus the new edition.

We hope the improvements in this edition substantially improve your experience with these life-changing ideas.

Joseph Grenny
Kerry Patterson
Ron McMillan
Al Switzler
Emily Gregory

crucial
conversations

1

WHAT'S A CRUCIAL CONVERSATION?

And Who Cares?

When people first hear the term "Crucial Conversation," many conjure up images of presidents, emperors, and prime ministers seated around a massive table while they debate the future. Although it's true that such discussions have a wide-sweeping impact, they're not the only kind we have in mind. Crucial Conversations happen to everyone. They're the daily conversations that reshape your life.

Now, what makes one of your conversations crucial as opposed to plain vanilla? First, *opinions vary*. For example, you're talking with your boss about a possible promotion. She thinks you're not ready; you think you are. Second, *stakes are high*. You're in a meeting with four coworkers, and you're trying to pick a new marketing strategy. You've got to do something different, or your company is in trouble. Third, *emotions run strong*. You're in the middle of a casual discussion with your spouse, and he or she brings up an "ugly incident" that took place at yesterday's neighborhood party. Apparently not only did you flirt with someone at the party, but according to your spouse, "You were practically making out." You don't remember flirting. You simply remember being polite and friendly. Your spouse walks off in a huff.

And speaking of the party, at one point during the evening you found yourself making small talk with the somewhat crotchety and colorful neighbor from an adjoining apartment. One minute he's telling you all about his shrinking kidneys; the next he's complaining about the smell of your previous night's dinner wafting through his vent. "I'm allergic to ginger, you know," he grouses. From that moment on, you end up in a heated debate over whether your right to stir-fry trumps the fact that smelling the spice makes his ears sweat. Not your most diplomatic moment. It escalates to shouting, and the neighbor finishes by threatening you with a culinary assault lawsuit while you storm off. Emotions were running *really* strong.

WHAT MAKES THESE CONVERSATIONS CRUCIAL?

What makes each of these conversations crucial—and not simply frustrating, frightening, or annoying—is that the outcome could have a huge impact on either relationships or results that affect you greatly.

In each of the above cases, some element of your daily routine could be forever altered for better or worse. Clearly a promotion could make a big difference. Your company's success affects you and everyone you work with. Your relationship with your spouse influences every aspect of your life. Even something as trivial as a debate over cooking smells can damage your quality of life.

These examples, of course, are merely the tip of an enormous and ugly iceberg of topics that can lead us into conversational disaster. Others include:

- Ending a relationship
- Talking to a coworker who makes offensive comments

- Asking a friend to repay a loan
- Giving the boss feedback about her behavior
- Approaching a boss who's breaking his own safety or quality policies
- Addressing racist or sexist behavior
- Critiquing a colleague's work
- Asking a roommate to move out
- Resolving custody or visitation issues with an ex
- Dealing with a rebellious teen
- Talking to a team member who isn't keeping commitments
- Discussing problems with sexual intimacy
- Confronting a loved one about a substance abuse problem
- Talking to a colleague who's hoarding information or resources
- Giving an unfavorable performance review
- Asking in-laws to quit interfering
- Talking to a coworker about a personal hygiene problem

These situations cause stress and strain in our lives, and one misstep in any of them could have huge consequences. But it doesn't have to be this way. If you know how to handle Crucial Conversations, you can effectively hold tough conversations about virtually any topic and resolve the situation. But that's not what typically happens.

Crucial Conversation (krōō shel kän´vŭr sa´ shen) *n*
A discussion between two or more people in which they hold
(1) opposing opinions about a (2) high-stakes issue and where
(3) emotions run strong. See Figure 1.1.

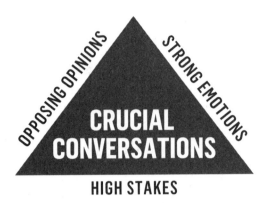

Figure 1.1   The definition of a Crucial Conversation

Lag Time Is a Factor

In each of these examples, the determining factor between success and failure is the amount of time that passes between when the problem emerges and when those involved find a way to honestly and respectfully resolve it. What we're suggesting is that the greatest damage to your relationship with your in-laws is not due to their occasional interference. It's the toxic emotions and dysfunctional behavior that occurs in the absence of a forthright conversation that causes the greatest damage. Biased behavior in your workplace is a problem, but its impact is multiplied when people fail to confront, discuss, and resolve the behavior. It's one thing to have a boss who fails to keep her commitments. It's another to have the problem fester into gossip, mistrust, and covert resentment as it echoes through hallways rather than being frankly addressed. The real damage happens during the lag time between people seeing her weaknesses and people addressing her weaknesses.

Think about relationships where the lag time between when you feel a problem and when you discuss it is short. Odds are that you would describe these relationships as characterized by trust, productivity, and intimacy. Now think about the reverse. Think about teams where it can take weeks, months, or years to honestly address the elephants in the room. What happens in the absence of candid dialogue? Contention. Resentment. Gamesmanship. Poor decisions. Spotty execution. Missed opportunities. *At the heart of almost all chronic problems in relationships, teams, organizations, and even nations are Crucial Conversations people either don't hold or don't hold well.* Decades of research have led us to conclude that:

> *You can measure the health of relationships, teams, and organizations by measuring the lag time between when problems are identified and when they are resolved.*

The only reliable path to resolving problems is to find the shortest path to effective conversation.

Why the Lag? How We Typically Handle Crucial Conversations

When we face Crucial Conversations, we have three broad options:

- We can avoid them.
- We can face them and handle them poorly.
- We can face them and handle them well.

That seems simple enough. Walk away from Crucial Conversations and suffer the consequences. Handle them poorly and suffer the consequences. Or handle them well, resolve the situation, and improve the relationship.

"I don't know," you think to yourself. "Given the three choices, I'll go with handling them well."

But do we handle them well? When talking turns tough, do we pause, take a deep breath, announce to our inner selves, "Uh-oh, this discussion is crucial. I'd better pay close attention," and then trot out our best behavior? Sometimes. Sometimes we boldly tackle hot topics, monitor our behavior, solve problems, and preserve relationships. Sometimes we're just flat-out *good*.

But all too often we fall into the other two camps. The lag time between identifying a problem and effectively resolving it grows because either we don't address it at all, or we address it poorly and the problem persists.

We Avoid Crucial Conversations

Despite the importance of Crucial Conversations, we often back away from them because we fear engaging will make matters worse. We become masters at avoiding tough conversations. Coworkers send emails when they should pick up the phone and talk openly. Bosses send texts rather than jumping on a video call. Family members change the subject when an issue gets too risky. We have one friend who learned from a Post-it note that his life partner of 17 years was leaving him. We use all kinds of tactics to dodge touchy issues.

Of course, there are risks in speaking up, especially to those with more power than you. But what few of us tend to be honest with ourselves about is the alternative to taking this risk. When it comes to Crucial Conversations, you have only two choices:

1. Talk it out.
2. Act it out.

If you fail to discuss issues you have with your boss, your life partner, your neighbor, or your peer, will those issues magically disappear? No. Instead, they will become the lens you see the other person through. And how you see always shows up in how you act. Your resentment will show up in how you treat the other person. For instance, you'll snap at the person, spend less time with him or her, be quicker to accuse the person of dishonesty or selfishness, or withhold information or affection. The problem will persist, and acting out your feelings instead of talking them out will add strain to an already crucial situation. The longer the lag time during which you act out your feelings rather than talk them out, the more damage you'll do to both relationships and results.

We Handle Them Poorly

On the flip side of avoidance, we have the problem of handling Crucial Conversations poorly. Often in these tough moments, we're at our absolute worst—we exaggerate; we yell; we withdraw; we say things we later regret. The sad irony of Crucial Conversations is that *when it matters most, we tend to do our worst.*

Why is that?

We're designed wrong. When conversations turn from routine to crucial, our instincts conspire against us. Strong emotions don't exactly prepare us to converse effectively. Countless generations of genetic shaping drive humans to react to interpersonal threats the same way we deal with physical ones. Our natural tendencies in moments that seem threatening lean toward fight or flight rather than listen and speak.

For instance, consider a typical Crucial Conversation. Someone says something you disagree with about a topic that matters a great deal to you, and your body registers the threat. Your body's instinct is to prepare you for physical safety. Two tiny organs seated neatly atop your kidneys pump adrenaline into your bloodstream. Your brain diverts blood from activities it deems nonessential (like thoughtfully and respectfully opening a conversation) to high-priority survival tasks (such as hitting and running). As the large muscles of the arms and legs get *more* blood, the higher-level reasoning sections of your brain get *less*. As a result, you end up facing challenging conversations with the same intellectual equipment available to a rodent. Your body is preparing to deal with an attacking saber-toothed tiger, not your boss, neighbor, or loved ones.

We're under pressure. Frequently, Crucial Conversations come out of nowhere. And since you're caught by surprise, you're forced to conduct an extraordinarily complex interaction in real time—no books, no coaches, and certainly no short breaks while a team of diplomats runs to your aid and pumps you full of suave ideas.

What *do* you have to work with? The issue at hand, the other person, and a brain that's drunk on adrenaline and almost incapable of rational thought. It's little wonder we often say and do things that make perfect sense in the moment but later on seem, well, stupid.

"What was I thinking?" you wonder—when what you should be asking is "What part of my brain was I thinking with?"

The truth is, you were trying to solve a complex interpersonal problem with a brain designed to do little more than assure your survival. You're lucky you didn't suffer a stroke.

We're stumped. We don't know where to start with approaching a Crucial Conversation effectively. We're making this up as we go along because few of us have seen real-life models of effective communication skills. Let's say that you actually planned for a tough conversation— maybe you've even mentally rehearsed. You feel prepared, and you're as cool as a cucumber. Will you succeed? Not if you haven't seen what true success looks like. Practice doesn't make perfect; *perfect* practice makes perfect.

This means that first you have to know what to practice. You've probably had ample opportunity to see what *not* to do—as modeled by friends, colleagues, and, yes, even your parents. In fact, you may have sworn time and again not to act the same way. You've watched your dad nod and sulk while his mother critiqued his life choices. Your mom taught you by example to respond to unkindness with biting sarcasm. And your first boss's favorite maxim was "If you can't say something nice, don't say anything at all." At least until the person he couldn't say something nice about left the room.

With no healthy models, what do you do? You do what most people do. You wing it. You piece together the words, try to make them sound nonthreatening, and hope the other person agrees with your perspective right away. But since you have no real idea of how to bring up the topic safely or respond to the other person's arguments, your attempts tend to fall short, and the lag time grows.

We act in self-defeating ways. Sometimes in our doped-up, dumbed-down state, the strategies we choose for dealing with our Crucial Conversations are perfectly designed to keep us from what we actually want. We're our own worst enemies. Here's how this works.

Let's say your significant other has been paying less and less attention to you. You realize he or she has a busy job, but you still would like more time together. You drop a few hints about the issue, but your loved one doesn't handle it well. You decide not to put on added pressure, so you clam up. Of course, since you're not all that happy with the arrangement, your displeasure now comes out through an occasional sarcastic remark: "Another late night, huh? I've got Facebook friends I feel closer to."

Unfortunately (and here's where the problem becomes self-defeating), the more you snip and snap, the less your loved one wants to be around you. So he or she spends less time with you, you become even more upset, and the spiral continues. Your behavior is now actually creating the very thing you didn't want in the first place. You're caught in an unhealthy, self-defeating loop.

Or maybe you have a roommate—we'll call him Terry—who shamelessly wears your and your other roommates' clothes without asking. In fact, one day while walking out the door, he glibly announces that he's wearing something from each of your closets. You see Taylor's pants, Scott's shirt, and even Chris's new matching shoes-and-socks ensemble. What of *yours* could he possibly be wearing? Eew!

Your response, quite naturally, is to bad-mouth Terry behind his back. That is, until one day when he overhears you belittling him to a friend. You're so embarrassed, you avoid being around him. And now when you're out of the apartment, he wears your clothes, eats your food, and uses your laptop out of spite.

Let's try another example. You're a woman on a project team run by a man. Over the past two months you've noticed that when men on the team offer ideas in brainstorming meetings, he responds with "Good comment" and a thoughtful nod. When a woman offers an idea, he rarely makes eye contact and offers a soft "OK." After the first meeting where it happened, you were curious. You had a sense that it would be helpful to call it to his attention; still, you decided against it for fear of offending him so early in the project. After you saw the behavior again in the second meeting, you were convinced not just that it was a pattern, but that he was likely incorrigible. By the eighth time you saw the pattern, you felt hot rage shoot through your spine. He has noted your sullen seething and has decided you either don't respect him or, worse, are actively undermining his project. Rather than exploring his concerns with you, he nurses them into a full-fledged indictment. As a result, he rarely looks in your direction during meetings and takes your potentially constructive comments as personal attacks.

In both cases, you're caught in a self-defeating loop. The more the two of you choose to continue your agitated silence, the more you both create the very behaviors the other despises.

In each of these examples of unhealthy downward spirals, the stakes were moderate to high, opinions differed, and emotions ran strong. In a couple of the examples, the stakes were fairly low at first, but with time and growing emotions, the relationships soured and quality of life suffered—driving the stakes up.

There Is Hope

So what's the solution to stepping up to these conversations and effectively resolving the situations before they drag out and grow to unmanageable levels?

The answer is to gain the skills needed to successfully address and resolve these relationships through Crucial Conversations. When you're confident in the skills you need, you won't hesitate to step up to these conversations. You'll know that a good outcome is possible, and you'll be able to create a scenario where everyone involved feels safe discussing his or her concerns. The rest of the book is concerned with teaching you skills to achieve these positive outcomes.

For now, let's look at how having those skills impacts every area of your life for the better.

 WORKING THROUGH DIVORCE

The skills you'll learn in this book will help you approach some of the most pivotal moments in your life. Coauthor Emily Gregory relied on these skills in the face of a life-changing decision, and they made all the difference. View her story in the video *Working Through Divorce* and learn about the power of Crucial Conversations skills at crucialconversations.com.

THE RESEARCH: HOW CRUCIAL CONVERSATIONS SKILLS IMPROVE YOUR LIFE

Strong relationships, careers, organizations, and communities all draw from the same source of power—the ability to talk openly about high-stakes, emotional, controversial topics.

The following is a small sampling of the decades of research that brought us to this important insight.

Increase Your Influence

Could the ability to master Crucial Conversations help your career? Absolutely. In a series of studies across 17 organizations, we identified thousands of what we call "opinion leaders." We'll cover more on what this term means in the next chapter. For now, just know that these were individuals who were admired by peers and bosses alike for their competence and insight. One of the most commonly cited skills people associated with them was their ability to raise emotionally and politically risky issues in a way that others couldn't. Colleagues envied their ability to speak truth to those in power. When people weren't sure how to let those in upper management know they were out of touch with reality, more often than not it was these skillful women and men who shrank the lag time.

We've all seen people hurt their careers by ineffectively discussing tough issues. You may have done it yourself. Fed up with a lengthy and unhealthy pattern of behavior, you finally speak out—but a bit too abruptly. Oops. Or maybe an issue becomes so hot that as your peers twitch and fidget themselves into a quivering mass of potential stroke victims, you decide to say something. It's not a pretty discussion—but somebody has to have the guts to keep the boss from doing something stupid. (Gulp.)

Without realizing it, from the time we are three or four years old, most of us come to the dangerous conclusion that we often have to choose between telling the truth and keeping a friend. Lag time becomes a way of life as we procrastinate, putting off conversations that might otherwise lead to resolution and stronger relationships. Instead, we build resentment and alienation as we act out rather than talk out our concerns.

People who routinely hold Crucial Conversations and hold them well are able to express controversial and even risky opinions in a way that gets heard. Their bosses, peers, and direct reports listen without becoming defensive or angry.

Time and again we've watched opinion leaders find ways to both tell the truth and keep relationships. We marveled as we watched them step up to conversations in ways that actually made working relationships stronger. We discovered that the only way to really strengthen relationships is *through* the truth, not *around* it.

What about *your* career? Are there Crucial Conversations that you're not holding or not holding well? Is this undermining your influence? And more importantly, would your career take a step forward if you could improve how you're dealing with these conversations?

Improve Your Organization

Is it possible that an organization's performance could hang on something as soft and gushy as how individuals deal with Crucial Conversations?

Study after study suggests that the answer is *yes*.

We began our work 30 years ago looking for what we called *crucial moments*. We wondered, "Are there a handful of moments when someone's actions *disproportionately affect* key performance indicators?" And if so, what are those moments, and how should we act when they occur?

It was that search that led us to Crucial Conversations. We've found that more often than not, the world changes when people have to deal with a very risky issue and either do it poorly or do it well. For example:

Silence kills. A doctor is getting ready to insert a central IV line into a patient but fails to put on the proper gloves, gown, and mask to ensure the procedure is done as safely as possible. After the nurse reminds the doctor of the proper protections, the doctor ignores her comment and begins the insertion. In a study of over 7,000 doctors and nurses, we've found caregivers face this crucial moment all the time. In fact, 84 percent of respondents said that they regularly see people taking shortcuts, exhibiting incompetence, or breaking rules.

And that's not the problem!

The real problem is that those who observe deviations or infractions *say nothing*. Across the world we've found that the odds of a nurse speaking up in this crucial moment are less than 1 in 12. The odds of doctors stepping up to similar Crucial Conversations aren't much better.

And when they don't speak up, when they don't hold an effective Crucial Conversation, it impacts critical results like patient safety, nursing turnover, physician satisfaction, and nursing productivity.

Silence fails. When it comes to the corporate world, the most common complaint of executives and managers is that their people work in silos. They are great at tasks they can handle entirely within their team. Unfortunately, close to 80 percent of the projects that require cross-functional cooperation *cost far more than expected, produce less than hoped for, and run significantly over budget*. We wondered why.

So we studied over 2,200 projects and programs that had been rolled out at hundreds of organizations worldwide. The findings were stunning. You can predict months or years in advance with nearly 90 percent accuracy which projects will fail. *The* predictor of success or failure was whether people could hold specific, relevant Crucial Conversations. For example, could they speak up if they thought the scope and schedule were unrealistic? Or did they go silent when a cross-functional team member began sloughing off? Or even more tricky—what should they do when an executive failed to provide leadership for the effort?

In most organizations we studied, employees fell silent when these crucial moments hit. Fortunately, in those organizations where people were able to candidly and effectively speak up about these concerns, the projects were less than half as likely to fail. When a project failed, problems showed up in key performance indicators such as spiraling costs, late delivery times, and low morale. But our research showed that the underlying cause was the unwillingness or inability to speak up at crucial moments.

———————

Other studies we've conducted show that companies with employees who are skilled at Crucial Conversations:

- Respond five times faster to financial downturns—and make budget adjustments far more intelligently—than less-skilled peers.
- Are two-thirds more likely to avoid injury and death due to unsafe conditions.
- Save over $1,500 and an eight-hour workday for every Crucial Conversation employees hold rather than avoid.
- Substantially increase trust and reduce transaction costs in virtual work teams. Those who can't handle their Crucial Conversations suffer (through backstabbing, gossip, undermining, passive aggression, etc.) up to three times more often in virtual teams than in colocated teams.
- Influence change in colleagues who are bullying, conniving, dishonest, or incompetent. When over 4,000 respondents were asked, 93 percent of them said that, in their organization, people like this are almost "untouchable"—staying in their position four years or longer without being held accountable.

Most leaders get it wrong. They think that organizational productivity and performance are simply about policies, processes, structures, or systems. So when their software product doesn't ship on time, they benchmark others' development processes. Or when productivity flags, they tweak their performance management system. When teams aren't cooperating, they restructure.

Our research shows that these types of nonhuman changes fail more often than they succeed. That's because the real problem lies not in implementing a new process, but in getting people to hold one another accountable to the process. And that requires Crucial Conversations skills.

In the *worst* companies, poor performers are first ignored and then transferred. In *good* companies, bosses eventually deal with problems. In the *best* companies, everyone holds everyone else accountable—regardless of level or position. The path to high productivity passes not through a static system, but through face-to-face conversations.

So what about you? Is your organization stuck in its progress toward some important goal? What is the typical lag time in your organization between identifying and discussing politically or emotionally risky issues? Do people step up to or walk away from Crucial Conversations? Could you take a big step forward by shrinking your typical lag time?

Strengthen Your Relationships

Could failed Crucial Conversations lead to failed relationships? When you ask the average person what causes couples to break up, he or she usually suggests that it's due to differences of opinion. You know, people have different preferences about managing their finances, spicing up their love lives, or rearing their children.

In truth, *everyone* argues about important issues. But not everyone splits up. It's *how* you argue that matters.

For example, when psychologist Howard Markman examined couples in the throes of heated discussions, he learned that people fall into three categories—those who digress into threats and name-calling, those who revert to silent fuming, and those who speak openly, honestly, and effectively.

After observing couples for hundreds of hours, Markman and his research partner Clifford Notarius predicted relationship outcomes and tracked their research subjects' relationships for the next decade. Remarkably, they predicted nearly 90 percent of the divorces that occurred.[1] But more importantly, they found that helping couples learn to hold Crucial Conversations more effectively reduced the chance of unhappiness or breakup by more than half!

Now what about you? Think of your own important relationships. Are there a few Crucial Conversations that you're currently avoiding or handling poorly? Do you walk away from some issues only to charge recklessly into others? Do you hold in ugly opinions only to have them tumble out as sarcastic remarks or cheap shots? When it matters the most (after all, these are your cherished loved ones), are you on your worst behavior? If so, you definitely have something to gain by learning more about how to handle Crucial Conversations.

Boost Your Personal Health

If the evidence so far isn't compelling enough, what would you say if we told you that the ability to master Crucial Conversations is a key to a healthier and longer life?

Immune systems. Consider the groundbreaking research done by Dr. Janice Kiecolt-Glaser and Dr. Ronald Glaser. They studied the immune systems of couples who had been married an average of 42 years by comparing those who argued constantly with those who resolved their differences effectively. It turns out that arguing for decades *doesn't* lessen the destructive blow of constant conflict. Quite the contrary. Those who routinely failed their Crucial Conversations had far weaker immune systems and worse health than those who found a way to resolve them well.[2]

Life-threatening diseases. In perhaps the most revealing of all the health-related studies, a group of subjects who had contracted malignant melanoma received traditional treatment and then were divided into two groups. One group met weekly for only six weeks; the other did not. Facilitators taught the first group of recovering patients specific communication skills.

After meeting only six times and then dispersing for five years, the subjects who learned how to express themselves effectively had a higher survival rate—only 9 percent succumbed as opposed to almost 30 percent in the untrained group.[3] Think about the implications of this study. Just a modest improvement in the ability to talk and connect with others corresponded to a two-thirds decrease in the death rate.

This study is just one sample of how the way you talk or don't talk can dramatically affect your health. Mountains of research suggest that the negative feelings we hold in and the emotional pain we suffer as we stumble our way through unhealthy conversations slowly eat away at our health. In some cases, the impact of failed conversations leads to minor problems. In others, it results in disaster. In all cases, failed conversations never make us happier, healthier, or better off.

———

So how about you? What are the specific conversations that gnaw at you the most? Which conversations (if you held them or improved them) would strengthen your immune system, help ward off disease, and increase your quality of life and well-being?

SUMMARY: WHAT'S A CRUCIAL CONVERSATION?

When stakes are high, opinions vary, and emotions start to run strong, casual conversations transform into crucial ones. Ironically, the more crucial the conversation, the less likely we are to handle it well. When we fail a Crucial Conversation, every aspect of our lives can be affected— from our companies, to our careers, to our communities, to our relationships, to our personal health. And the longer the lag time, the more room for mischief.

But there is good news. As we learn how to step up to Crucial Conversations—and handle them well—with one set of high-leverage skills we can influence virtually every domain of our lives.

What is this all-important skill set? What do people who sail through Crucial Conversations actually do? More importantly, can we do it too?

2

MASTERING CRUCIAL CONVERSATIONS

The Power of Dialogue

To be honest, we didn't *study* our way into a discovery of Crucial Conversations. Instead, we *stumbled* into it.

Over the years, we worked with dozens of leaders in a variety of industries who were trying to implement dramatic changes. Part of our consulting methodology involved helping them find opinion leaders embedded throughout their organizations who might be helpful in the effort. We did so in a pretty straightforward way. First, we asked people to name the two or three people they turned to first when they were struggling to get something done. Over the past decades, we've asked tens of thousands of people to identify the individuals in their organizations who knew how to make things happen when others felt stymied. We wanted to find those who were not just influential, but *far more* influential than the rest.

Each time, as we compiled the names into a list, a pattern emerged. Lots of people were named by one or two colleagues. Some found their way onto five or six lists. These were people who were *good* at influence, but not good enough to be widely identified as top opinion leaders. And then there were the handful who were named 30 or more times. These were the *best*—the ones who could make big things happen in their areas. Some were managers and supervisors. Many were not.

One of the opinion leaders we became particularly interested in meeting was named Kevin. He was the only one of eight vice presidents in his company to be identified as exceedingly influential. We wanted to know why. So we watched him at work.

At first, Kevin didn't do anything remarkable. In truth, he looked like every other VP. He answered his phone, talked to his direct reports, and continued about his pleasant, but routine, routine.

THE STARTLING DISCOVERY

After trailing Kevin for almost a week, we began to wonder if he really did act in ways that set him apart from others or if his influence was simply a matter of popularity. And then we followed Kevin into a meeting.

Kevin, his peers, and their boss were deciding on a new location for their offices—would they move across town, across the state, or across the country? The first two execs presented their arguments for their top choices, and as expected, their points were greeted by penetrating questions from the full team. No vague claim went unclarified, no unsupported reasoning unquestioned.

Then Chris, the CEO, pitched his preference—one that was both unpopular and potentially disastrous. However, when people tried to disagree or push back, Chris responded poorly. Since he was the big boss, he didn't exactly have to browbeat people to get what he wanted. Instead, he became slightly defensive. First he raised an eyebrow. Then he raised his finger. Finally he raised his voice—just a little. It wasn't long until people stopped questioning him, and Chris's inadequate proposal was quietly accepted.

Well almost. That's when Kevin spoke up. His words were simple enough—something like, "Hey, Chris, can I check something out with you?"

The reaction was stunning—everyone in the room stopped breathing. But Kevin ignored the apparent terror of his colleagues and plunged on ahead. In the next few minutes he in essence told the CEO that he appeared to be violating his own decision-making guidelines. He was subtly using his power to move the new offices to his hometown.

Kevin continued to explain what he saw happening, and when he finished the first minutes of this delicate exchange, Chris was quiet for a moment. Then he nodded. "You're absolutely right," he finally concluded. "I have been trying to force my opinion on you. Let's back up and try again."

This was a Crucial Conversation, and Kevin played no games whatsoever. He didn't resort to silence like his colleagues, nor did he try to force his arguments on others. Somehow he managed to achieve absolute candor, but he did so in a way that showed deep respect for Chris. It was a remarkable thing to watch. As a result, the team chose a far more effective location, and Kevin's boss appreciated his caring coaching.

When Kevin was done, one of his peers turned to us and said, "Did you see how he did that? If you want to know how he gets things done, figure out what he just did."

So we did. In fact, we spent the next 30 years discovering what Kevin and people like him do. What typically set them apart from the rest of the pack was their ability to avoid what we came to call the "Fool's Choice."

You see, Kevin's contribution was not his insight. Almost everyone could see what was happening. People knew they were allowing themselves to be steamrolled into making a bad decision. But all of them except for Kevin believed they had to make a choice between two bad alternatives:

- **Option 1.** Speak up and turn the most powerful person in the company into their sworn enemy.
- **Option 2.** Suffer in silence and make a bad decision that might ruin the company.

The mistake most of us make in our Crucial Conversations is we believe that we have to choose between telling the truth and keeping a friend. As we suggested in the previous chapter, we begin believing in the Fool's Choice from an early age. For instance, we learned that when Grandma served an enormous wedge of her famous brussels-sprouts pie à la mode and then asked, "Do you like it?" she *really* meant, "Do you like *me*?" When we answered honestly and saw the look of hurt and horror on her face, we made a decision that affected the rest of our lives: "From this day forward, I will be alert for moments when I must choose between candor and kindness."

BEYOND THE FOOL'S CHOICE

And from that day forward, we found plenty of those moments—with bosses, colleagues, loved ones, and line cutters. Drawing out lag time became a way of life, and the consequences followed.

That's why our research with Kevin (and hundreds of individuals like him) was so important. We discovered a core group of human beings who refused to make the Fool's Choice. Their goal was different from your average person's. When Kevin spoke up, his implicit question was, "How can I be 100 percent honest with Chris and at the same time be 100 percent respectful?"

Following that consequential meeting, we began looking for more Kevins, and we found them all over the world. We found them in industry, government, academia, and nonprofit organizations. They were fairly easy to locate because they were almost always among the most influential employees in their organizations. Not only did they refuse to make the Fool's Choice, but they were also far more skilled in how they acted than their colleagues.

But what exactly did they do? Kevin wasn't *that* different from his colleagues. Could what he did be learned by others?

To answer this question, let's first explore what Kevin was able to *achieve*. This will help us see where we're trying to go. Then we'll examine the tools that effective communicators routinely use and learn to apply them to our own Crucial Conversations.

DIALOGUE

When it comes to Crucial Conversations, skilled people find a way to get all relevant information (from themselves and others) out into the open.

That's it. At the core of every successful conversation lies the free flow of information. People openly and honestly express their opinions, share their feelings, and articulate their theories. They willingly and capably share their views, even when their ideas are controversial or unpopular. It's the one thing that Kevin and the other extremely effective communicators we studied were routinely able to achieve.

What they do is effectively create a dialogue.

---

di·a·logue or **di·a·log** (dī′ ∂-lôg″, -lòg) *n*
The free flow of meaning between two or more people.

As we talk about dialogue, we're faced with two questions. First, how does this free flow of meaning lead to success? Second, what can you do to encourage meaning to flow freely?

We'll explain the relationship between the free flow of meaning and success in this chapter. The second question—what must you do in order to achieve dialogue when it matters the most?—will take us the rest of the book to answer.

Filling the Pool of Shared Meaning

Each of us enters conversations with our own thoughts and feelings about the topic at hand. This unique combination makes up our personal pool of meaning. This pool not only informs us, but also propels our every action.

When two or more of us enter Crucial Conversations, by definition we don't share the same pool. Our opinions differ. I believe one thing; you another. I have one history; you another.

People who are skilled at dialogue do their best to make it safe for everyone to add meaning to the *shared* pool—even ideas that at first glance appear controversial or wrong. Obviously, everyone doesn't agree with every idea; people simply do their best to ensure that all ideas find their way into the open.

As the Pool of Shared Meaning grows, it helps people in two ways. First, as individuals are exposed to more accurate and relevant information, they make better choices. In a very real sense, the Pool of Shared Meaning is a measure of a group's IQ. The larger the shared pool, the smarter the decisions.

On the other hand, we've all seen what happens when the shared pool is dangerously shallow. When people purposely withhold meaning from one another, individually *smart* people can do collectively *stupid* things.

For example, a client of ours shared the following story:

A woman checked into the hospital to have a tonsillectomy, and the surgical team erroneously removed a portion of her foot. How could this tragedy happen? In fact, why is it that nearly 22,000 hospital deaths in the United States each year stem from human error?[1] In part, because many healthcare professionals are afraid to speak their minds. In this case, no fewer than seven people wondered why the surgeon was working on the foot, but said nothing. Meaning didn't flow freely because people were afraid to speak up.

Of course, hospitals don't have a monopoly on fear. In every instance where bosses are smart, highly paid, confident, and outspoken (i.e., most of the world), people tend to hold back their opinions rather than risk angering someone in a position of power.

On the other hand, when people feel comfortable speaking up and meaning does flow freely, the shared pool can dramatically increase a group's ability to make better decisions. Consider what happened to Kevin's group. As everyone on the team began to explain his or her opinion, people formed a clearer and more complete picture of the circumstances.

As they began to understand the whys and wherefores of different proposals, they built off one another. Eventually, as one idea led to the next and then to the next, they came up with an alternative that no one had originally thought of and that all wholeheartedly supported. As a result of the free flow of meaning, the whole (final choice) was truly greater than the sum of the original parts. In short: *The Pool of Shared Meaning is the birthplace of synergy.*

As people sit through an open discussion, they understand why the shared solution is the best option, and they're committed to act. Kevin and the other VPs didn't buy into their final choice simply because they were involved; they bought in because they understood.

Conversely, when people aren't involved, when they sit back during touchy conversations, they're rarely committed to the final decision. Since their ideas remain in their heads and their opinions never make it into the pool, they end up quietly criticizing and passively resisting. Similarly, when others force their ideas into the pool, people have a hard time accepting the information. They may *say* they're on board but then walk away and follow through halfheartedly.

To quote Samuel Butler, "He that complies against his will is of his own opinion still."

The time you spend up front establishing a shared pool of meaning is more than paid for by faster, more unified, and more committed action later on.

For example, if Kevin and the other leaders had not been committed to their relocation decision, terrible consequences would have followed. Some people would have agreed to move; others would have dragged their feet. Some would have held heated discussions in the hallways. Others would have said nothing and then quietly fought the plan. More likely than not, the team would have been forced to meet again, discuss again, and decide again—since only one person favored the decision and the decision affected everyone.

Don't get us wrong. We're not suggesting that every decision be made by consensus or that the boss shouldn't take part in or even make the final choice. We're simply suggesting that whatever the decision-making method, the greater the shared meaning in the pool, the better the choice, the more the unity, and the stronger the conviction—whoever makes the choice.

Every time we find ourselves arguing, running away, or otherwise acting in an ineffective way, it's because we don't know how to share meaning. Instead of engaging in healthy dialogue, we play costly games.

For instance, sometimes we move to silence. We play Salute and Stay Mute. That is, we don't confront people in positions of authority. Or at home we may play Freeze Your Lover. With this tortured technique, we give loved ones the cold shoulder in order to get them to treat us better (what's the logic in that?).

Sometimes we rely on hints, sarcasm, innuendo, and looks of disgust to make our points. We play the martyr and then pretend we're actually trying to help. Or maybe, afraid to confront an individual, we blame an entire team for a problem—hoping the message will hit the right target. Whatever the technique, the overall method is the same. We withhold meaning from the pool. We go to silence.

On other occasions, not knowing how to stay in dialogue, we try to force our meaning into the pool. We rely on emotional violence— anything from verbal sniping, to intellectual bullying, to outright verbal attacks. We act like we know everything, hoping people will believe our arguments. We discredit others. We use force to get our way. We borrow power from the boss; we hit people with biased monologues; we make hurtful comments. The goal of all these behaviors is the same—to compel others to our point of view.

So to sum up: When stakes are high, opinions vary, and emotions run strong, we're often at our worst. In order to move to our best, we have to find a way to explain what is in each of our personal pools of meaning—especially our high-stakes, sensitive, and controversial thoughts and opinions—and to get others to share their pools. To achieve this, we have to develop the tools that make it safe for us to discuss these issues and to come to a *shared* pool of meaning.

DIALOGUE SKILLS ARE LEARNABLE

Here's the *really* good news. The skills for mastering high-stakes interactions are quite easy to spot and moderately easy to learn. A well-handled Crucial Conversation all but leaps out at you. When you see someone enter the dangerous waters of a high-stakes, emotional, controversial discussion and do a particularly good job, your natural reaction is to step back in awe. What starts as a doomed discussion ends up with a healthy resolution. It can take your breath away.

More important, not only are dialogue skills easy to spot, but they're also fairly easy to learn. That's where we're going next. We've isolated and captured the skills of the dialogue-gifted over decades of research. First, we followed around Kevin and others like him. When conversations turned *crucial*, we took detailed notes. Afterward, we compared our observations, tested our hypotheses, and honed our models until we found the skills that consistently explain the success of brilliant communicators. Finally, we combined our theories, models, and skills into a package of learnable tools—tools for talking when stakes are high. We then taught these skills and watched as key performance indicators and relationships improved.

Now we're ready to share what we've learned. Stay with us as we explore how to transform Crucial Conversations from frightening events into interactions that yield success and results. It's the most important set of skills you'll ever master.

My Crucial Conversation: Bobby R.

My Crucial Conversation began on the night before my first deployment to Iraq in 2004. There was a lot of tension between members of my family caused by past events and conflicting perspectives. The stress of my leaving to combat only increased the tension. On that night, one well-intended but deeply loaded question from my father sent me through the roof. The way I reacted over the next couple of hours started a downward spiral that affected my entire family. Siblings, cousins, aunts, uncles, parents, children, and grandparents all took sides.

My family ties continued to unravel as I led a platoon of soldiers through the streets of Baghdad. My wife was home with our one-year-old and pregnant with our second. During my tour, additional family encounters only worsened the situation, and after fourteen months of combat, I came home to a family that was completely broken at every existing generation. The silence between me and my father continued for five years.

Crucial Conversations saved my relationship with my parents. A neighbor who is a Crucial Conversations trainer invited me to his class before my third tour in Iraq. A couple of weeks before I deployed, I reached out to my father to let him know about the two children he had never seen and that I was leaving for combat. I told him I couldn't make the same mistake I had made five years earlier, and we agreed to meet.

On a beautiful sunset balcony in Houston, my dad and I spent three tense hours dealing with a lot of pain and built-up resentment. I kept in mind what I had been taught and, rather than compromising candor, tried my best to create conditions where we could be both honest and respectful. It was incredibly difficult. Sometimes the honesty threatened to put us right back in the angry state that got us there. But I kept focusing on what I really wanted—a relationship with my family.

At the end of the conversation, we met my mom for dinner. She had been the most hurt by my anger in the past and was skeptical. She was sure I was still the argumentative, sarcastic, spiteful, and arrogant child of my youth. She gave me a chance based on my father's assessment of my respect, remorse, and clear demonstration of Mutual Purpose. I am now in a loving relationship with my wife, four children, and parents. We have agreed to never bury our concerns in silence again.

I attribute the relationship I have today to the success of that one Crucial Conversation on the balcony. Had I not practiced what I had learned, my relationship with my father would have died from anger and indifference. That conversation happened because of a friend who introduced me to Crucial Conversations.

HERE'S WHERE WE'RE GOING

Throughout the remainder of the book, we'll explore the tools people use to help create the conditions of dialogue. While Crucial Conversations rarely follow a neat path, the principles and skills we will share are generally applied in a predictable order. For example, Part I of the book ("What to Do Before You Open Your Mouth") describes the "preparation principles"—the things we need to do before we begin to ensure we are primed for an effective conversation. And there is little chance of healthy dialogue if you don't focus on the right problem (Chapter 3, "Choose Your Topic"), get your motives right (Chapter 4, "Start with Heart"), and manage your emotions (Chapter 5, "Master My Stories").

Part II is called "How to Open Your Mouth." Here we'll teach you to recognize early signs of problems (Chapter 6, "Learn to Look"). Next we'll share how to create the key condition that allows you to talk with almost anyone about almost anything: *safety* (Chapter 7, "Make It Safe"). We then get tactical, teaching strategies for sharing your views in a way that is both truthful and least likely to provoke defensiveness (Chapter 8, "STATE My Path") and for helping others to productively express their views as well (Chapter 9, "Explore Others' Paths"). Then we take you to a remarkable place in the US Rocky Mountains where we learn lessons for minimizing the misery we feel when receiving tough feedback (Chapter 10, "Retake Your Pen").

In Part III ("How to Finish"), we'll share two important tools for finishing strong (Chapter 11, "Move to Action").

As you read on (Chapter 12, "Yeah, But"), you will learn the key skills of talking, listening, and acting together in a way that improves both relationships and results.

Finally, we'll tie all the theories and skills together (Chapter 13, "Putting It All Together") by providing both a model and an extended example. We are confident that as you not only read but practice what you learn, *you will gain greater and greater confidence in talking when stakes are high.*

SUMMARY: MASTERING CRUCIAL CONVERSATIONS

When facing a Crucial Conversation, most of us unconsciously make a "Fool's Choice"—we think we have to choose between "telling the truth" and "keeping a friend." Skilled communicators resist this false tradeoff and look for ways to do both. They look for a way to be both 100 percent honest and 100 percent respectful at the same time. In short, they look for way to get to dialogue: a condition where meaning flows freely between parties resulting in a larger pool of information shared by all.

A larger shared pool of meaning leads to better decisions, better relationships, and more unified action. The remainder of this book shares learnable skills designed to help you get to dialogue during your most crucial moments.

PART I

WHAT TO DO BEFORE YOU OPEN YOUR MOUTH

Seventy percent of the success of a Crucial Conversation happens in your head, not through your mouth. The skills in this section are the prerequisites of success. Get these right, and the right words will often flow naturally from you. Ignore these, and no amount of technique or artifice will be enough to compensate.

In this section you'll learn how to be sure you're talking about the right things (Chapter 3, "Choose your Topic"), how to get your motives right (Chapter 4, "Start with Heart"), and how to understand and manage your own emotions when they're getting in the way of dialogue (Chapter 5, "Master My Stories").

3

CHOOSE YOUR TOPIC

How to Be Sure You Hold the Right Conversation

The moment you open your mouth to hold a Crucial Conversation, you've already made a decision—you've decided what to talk about. One of the biggest mistakes we make is assuming that just because we're talking, we must be solving the right problem. It's not that simple. If you're not addressing the *right* issue, you'll end up in the same conversation over and over again.

CRUCIAL CONVERSATIONS ARE "TOPIC-RICH" ENVIRONMENTS

Human interactions and relationships are complex. There are multiple issues and side issues and tangents. You've probably been in that conversation before. You think you're talking with your brother about plans for an upcoming family gathering. Suddenly, you're in a completely different conversation about the time your parents bought you a brand-new bike because you have always been their favorite and your brother could never measure up. Whoa, you think, where did that all come from?

Crucial Conversations are most successful when they're focused on one issue. Because human interactions are inherently complex, focusing a Crucial Conversation on a single topic takes effort. It requires us to thoughtfully unbundle and then prioritize the issues at hand.

For example, let's look at the case of Wendy and Sandrine. Wendy is a project manager at a global technology company. She's been there many years and has successfully led numerous projects, large and small. She recently began working with a new manager, Sandrine. Sandrine joined the organization a year ago with a reputation as a hard-charging, get-things-done, break-eggs-when-needed executive. Sandrine asked Wendy to put together a timeline for a new project, and now they're sitting down to review it.

> **Sandrine:** *I'm excited to have you and your team dig in on this project. Let's talk timelines.*

> **Wendy:** *It'll take us just over six months.*

> **Sandrine:** *Oh . . . Well . . . when I looked at it, it seemed like you should be able to finish the whole thing by the end of this quarter.*

At this point, we have the first element of a Crucial Conversation—a difference of opinion. Wendy thinks the project will take at least twice as long as Sandrine expected.

> **Wendy:** *Well it's a good thing we're talking about it now before we've made any commitments, because there's no way to finish it by then. I mean, that's half the usual time for a project like this.*

Sandrine: *That's why I put you in this role in the first place. You are able to do the impossible. Let me give you the full context of just how important this is. I need you to figure out how to get this done by the end of the quarter. Other project launches are at stake. The accelerated schedules are already in the master plan. Our senior team is counting on us. Or, more specifically, on* you.

And just like that, the next two elements of a Crucial Conversation come into play. The stakes are high, and emotions are rising. This is an important project—for Wendy, for Sandrine, and for their organization. Sandrine is feeling pressured and is starting to apply that same pressure on Wendy.

So what happens next?

Wendy: *Wait a minute . . . you've already made a commitment? You agreed to a deadline before we even talked about whether it was doable?*

Sandrine: *Hey, Wendy, you know we need a big win this year. Look, I really pushed for you to be the one to lead this project. Do you know what I said about you? I said you were a team player. Was I mistaken?*

Wow! There is a lot going on in this one conversation. Wendy has put together a timeline, shared it with her manager, and bam! The whole thing has blown up in her face. Not only does she still have to get to agreement with her manager about the project timeline (the original issue), but now there are a whole host of other issues as well. Think about what would be going through your mind right now if you were Wendy. For example:

- "How will I ever get this project done?"
- "She's setting me up to fail!"
- "This is unfair to my team!"
- "What am I going to say to my family about the crazy long hours I will be putting in?"
- "Can I tell the truth about what I'm thinking right now? Will I lose my job if I do?"
- "Do I even want this career? Do I want to work for Sandrine?"

Wendy is clearly facing a Crucial Conversation right now. But the question is, which conversation? What should she, right now in this moment with Sandrine, talk about?

WHY WE USUALLY CHOOSE THE WRONG TOPIC

When faced with complex problems like this, we rarely stop and ponder which topic we should address. Instead, we naturally default to one of two mistaken directions:

Easy over hard. When faced with a high-stakes, emotional conversation, we have a bias for choosing the topic we think we can win with. That usually means we pick something easier than the issue that is really in the way of our most important goals. We think, "I'll just start with this little issue and see how that goes." It's like we're testing the waters. Or trying to get across the lake without getting wet. For example, if you've concluded your direct report is incompetent at some aspect of his or her job, you might sugarcoat the problem by addressing minor recent mistakes. Your unstated hope is that your report will infer how big the problem is without your coming out and saying it. Nice try. But easy rarely works.

Recent over right. We tend to focus on the most recent event or behavior rather than on the one that matters the most. If a colleague treats your comments in meetings in a way you find disrespectful, you talk about the most recent slight rather than sharing the larger pattern. "Hey," you say after the meeting, "you started talking over me in there when I hadn't finished my point."

Your colleague shrugs and says, "Shoot. Sorry. I guess I got a little too enthusiastic." You *say*, "Uh-huh." But you *think*, "You do that all the time, you self-centered jerk!"

We favor recent over right for a couple of reasons. First, we can actually remember the specifics. Second, we don't want to be accused of dredging up ancient history.

Three Signs You're Having the Wrong Conversation

Falling into these traps leads to fairly predictable results. We end up having the wrong conversation, which keeps us stuck.

To avoid this mistake, learn to recognize three signals that you're talking about the wrong thing. Memorize them. When you see them, imagine a yellow warning light flashing in your mind that says, "Wrong topic!" When that light pulses, push back from the table and ask yourself, "What's the real issue here?"

1. **Your emotions escalate.** When you're having the wrong conversation, even if that conversation is going well, you know on some level that you're not addressing or resolving the issue. Consequently, you come in feeling frustrated, and that feeling increases as the conversation progresses. That's happening right now to Wendy in the conversation above. When the conversation started, she was feeling confident in her timeline. By the end, she was apprehensive and afraid for her job. That escalated emotion should signal to her that

the issue is no longer the project deadline. Something more important needs to be addressed!

2. **You walk away skeptical.** Sure, maybe you come to the end of the conversation with an agreement, but even as you walk away, you think to yourself, "Nothing is going to really change here." Or you get to agreement but doubt that the changes you settled on will solve the *real* problem. Whatever agreement you came to is only so much window dressing because it won't get you to what you really want.

3. **You're in a dèjá vu dialogue.** If you ever have the same conversation with the same people a second time, the problem is not *them*. It's *you*. You're having the wrong conversation. If even as you say the words they feel familiar because you've had this conversation before—maybe even a dozen times—you're on the wrong topic.

One of the best ways to ensure you talk about the right topic is to get good at noticing when you're on the wrong one. Memorize these three warning signs. Then every time you recognize they are happening, use them as a cue to push back from the table and ask yourself, "What's the real issue I need to address?"

SKILLS FOR FINDING THE RIGHT TOPIC

You've likely known someone who seems gifted at putting a finger on exactly the right issue. The conversation is swirling and churning, and suddenly the person says, "You know, I think the real issue here is *trust*. We've lost confidence in each other," or makes some other brilliant deduction of the previous 53 minutes of chaos. A dozen heads nod, and suddenly you begin making progress because you're now talking about the real issue. How does someone do that?

The answer is that this person is skilled at three elements of choosing the right topic. The person knows how to *unbundle, choose,* and *simplify* the issues involved.

Let's look first at unbundling.

Unbundle

There are three levels of conversations you may need to have about the issue itself, and a fourth relating to the process of the conversation—we'll address process later. A good way to find the right one begins by unbundling, or teasing apart, the various issues level by level. You can remember these levels with the acronym CPR.

Content. The first time a problem comes up, talk about the content—the immediate pain. If either the action itself or its immediate consequences are the issue, you've got a content problem. For example, your coworker failed to get you the marketing analytics you needed in order to finish a report for your manager. Now your neck is on the line because your report was late. Or you're giving a presentation in a team meeting, and one of your fellow team members keeps interrupting and talking over you. If this is the first time this has happened, it's a content problem.

Pattern. The next time the same problem comes up, think pattern. Now the concern is not just that this has happened once, but that a pattern is starting to develop, or already has. For example, the last three times a really exciting project came to your team, your manager assigned it to others despite your expressed interest. The issue is no longer just one assignment; it's the pattern that's emerging.

It can be challenging to determine when to move from content to pattern. Often, it may feel like you're jumping to conclusions if you move to pattern after only a second occurrence of the issue. Yet you want to address patterns early and candidly, before they become entrenched. It can be helpful to think of it this way: The first time something happens, it's an incident. The second time it might be coincidence. The third time, it's a pattern.

Relationship. Finally, as problems continue, they can begin to impact the relationship. Relationship issues get to deeper concerns about *trust*, *competence*, or *respect*. For example, we may begin to doubt someone's competence or question whether we can trust a person to keep commitments. Or we may conclude after repeated incidents that a person doesn't respect our role or contribution. With these doubts and questions at the forefront of our thinking, we begin to (subtly or overtly) relate to them differently. Sometimes a relationship issue can emerge fully formed in the first instance. For example, if you see a colleague put sensitive files onto a thumb drive and take the drive home, you may have an immediate trust issue.

To see CPR in action, let's take a look at a very sensitive example from a client of ours. How would you use CPR to help him decide what topic to address?

> *I am the only nonwhite person on my team. I have been called by the wrong name multiple times in meetings by my immediate manager. After it happened three times, I corrected her in the meeting. She later gave me feedback that I shouldn't have bothered to correct my name because all names of people of my ethnicity sound similar, so it shouldn't really make a difference to me. On another occasion she suggested I adopt an "English" name.*

Can you see how important it is for this person to decide what the right topic is to address? Unbundling helps people see a variety of options:

1. **Keep it at content.** Solve the immediate problem by correcting anyone who calls you by the wrong name. Or thank your manager for the suggestion, but let her know you would like to be called by your given name.
2. **Move to pattern.** Express your concern that her referring to you by wrong names has become a pattern.
3. **Talk relationship.** Let your manager know that your name is an important part of your identity, and that you feel disrespected when someone you work with regularly doesn't take the time to learn it. Or perhaps even more important, you feel disrespected by the suggestion that you change it.

Unbundling the issues with CPR helps us gain clarity into the situation. It also sets us up to make a conscious choice—at which level do we want to hold this conversation? Before we get to making that decision, though, let's consider one more issue you may want to discuss—the process of the conversation itself.

Do You Need to Talk About Process?

CPR is a powerful entry point as we begin to unravel complex interactions and consider the issues that are keeping us stuck. But not every issue fits neatly into content, pattern, and relationship. Occasionally you'll need to extend your conversation to cover the issue of the process of how we are discussing issues.

For example, years ago we were coaching a senior leader, Kayla, on her management style. She had a team of a dozen or so people, including an administrative assistant, April. April was fairly new to the team, and Kayla was eager to develop a good working relationship with her. Being new, April had some things to learn, and Kayla was quick, direct, and respectful in her feedback. Despite Kayla's skill in delivering feedback and coaching, April almost inevitably became defensive. Kayla tried everything we taught her about saying things in a way that would make it safe for April to hear her (skills you'll learn in later chapters). It just wasn't working.

After observing a few interactions, we suggested to Kayla that this was a process problem. Something about the process of how she was delivering feedback and how April was hearing it was creating the issue that was keeping them stuck. Kayla decided to make that the topic of her conversation. She set up a time to talk with April about how they were working together and how she, Kayla, could best provide feedback to April. She explained her intent: She wanted them to be able to work well together, and she wanted to see April succeed. That's why she gave feedback. Kayla shared (using the skills in this book) that she had noticed April's defensiveness and wanted to talk about a better process for delivering feedback.

The conversation went well. The two were able to come to some concrete agreements about how Kayla could deliver feedback to April in a way that April could and would hear it. And April committed to expressing her emotions in ways that worked better for Kayla.

Taking time to address the process of *how* we are communicating is especially important when there are differences in our communication styles or when our mode of communication changes from what we're used to.

Process issues often come into play across cultures as well. For example, we work with colleagues across Europe and Asia, teaching Crucial Conversations skills. While the principles are the same, there are clear and obvious variations in the ways people communicate in different cultures. One of our Dutch colleagues shared this experience of working with one of our Asian colleagues:

I wanted to have a good and honest conversation about some problems we were having working together. When I invited him to share his thoughts about the situation, he hardly said a word. The conversation was a disaster. Afterwards I sent him an email explaining that I thought the conversation was unsuccessful and that I really want to find a solution that we both felt good about. Later we had a new conversation, but this time about process rather than specific problems. I asked what I could have done differently. He shared with me that in his culture, he is not used to talking explicitly about what went wrong. My direct reference to our problems felt disrespectful. He said that for him, it was customary to begin by talking about how we are doing, family, and other such topics. From a Dutch perspective I was doing just fine. Having a process conversation helped me learn how to make my real intentions clearer to my colleague.

Process conversations are also especially important in relationships that are largely or exclusively virtual. When contact is infrequent, it's essential to talk explicitly about how you will communicate. For example, how will you make sure that everyone has a turn to speak? How will you make space for people to pause and think? What tools will you use? What norms should we establish? How will you accommodate different time zones and work patterns? To answer these questions, start by asking yourself, "When do virtual conversations work well for me? And when do they not?" Then, consider the process. Remember, if you don't talk it out, you'll act it out. And virtual relationships leave much more room for acting it out!

Choose

The next step in finding the right topic to discuss is to *choose*. Choosing is a matter of filtering all the issues you've teased apart through a single question: "What do I really want?" (You'll see even more of the power of this question in the next chapter.)

Ponder what your highest priority is; then choose the issue that stands between you and that objective. For example, if what you really want is to solve a customer problem, you may choose to deal with the content issue ("How do we get this to Malaysia in two days?") rather than the relationship ("I don't trust that you will handle this right") or pattern ("Our fulfillment team frequently puts off doing things until they become crises") issues. You choose to return to the other conversations later.

Simplify

Having made your choice, be sure you can state simply what you want to discuss. We're not talking about how you'll start the conversation. We mean narrow the problem down to a succinct statement. This is harder than it sounds. Try stopping people who are great during Crucial Conversations right before they address a concern (we've done this). Ask them, "What's the issue you want to address?" You'll find that they take far fewer words to say it than the rest of us. The more words it takes you to describe the topic, the less prepared you are to talk. For example, when we asked one skilled person what his message was in a forthcoming performance review, he said, "I've concluded he is not good at managing people or projects." Boom! Crystal clear. Simple. He's ready.

Why is this clarity so rare? Often when we mortals take this step, we feel a sense of dread. As we start to admit the real problem to ourselves, we panic about *how* we could possibly say it. It's less scary when we leave the problem vague. When you can slosh around an issue in a giant bowl of words, it's easy to water it down. But when you simply state the essence of what you need to address, you feel a jolting sense of accountability to do so. You stare the size of the issue square in the face.

But that shouldn't create panic. It should create resolution. Notice that the panic happens only when you conflate two problems. While part of your brain considers "*What's* the real issue?" another part shrieks, "*How* in the world will I say that?" Don't do this! If you worry about the *how* while trying to be honest about the *what*, you'll be tempted to water down your message. When that happens, "I don't think you are capable of managing people or projects" starts to sound like "How do *you* think things went on the product launch?" We mince words, dance around, and sugarcoat our way into the conversation.

Creating a simple problem sentence helps you both start with a clear purpose and hold yourself accountable. It gives you a standard by which to measure whether you told your full truth. Don't worry about how you'll say it. Just tell yourself the truth about what you want to say.

Having done that, you can address the next problem: "How can I both tell the truth *and* strengthen the relationship?" The next few chapters will help you address that challenge.

But put that on the shelf for now. At this point, just worry about getting the *what* right. Tell yourself the truth.

This can be tough. But self-honesty is the precondition to honesty with others. Let's say, for example, you and your colleagues are talking about where to place a group of new interns in your company. In the middle of the discussion about one of the interns, a peer volunteers, "There's a lot of Asians in our data analysis team, let's put him there." You're suddenly seized by two competing feelings: rage and terror. You're offended because you think the comment is either stupid or racist—or both. But you're scared because you can't imagine a way of addressing the issue without provoking a fight. You're tempted to simply stay in the content. Offer other options for the intern. Make an argument about why other areas would be better for him. All the while the real concern is simmering inside you.

What should you do? To begin with, tell yourself the truth. Even if you don't know what to say in the moment, stop and clarify what is truly bothering you. Only then can you decide what the right next step is. Having told yourself the truth (you believe his comment is evidence of either subtle or egregious racism), you can then decide if, when, and how to have that conversation.

A WORD OF WARNING: BE ALERT TO WHEN THE TOPIC CHANGES

Most of the crucial problems we face require us to address issues at the pattern, process, or relationship level. Very rarely is a content issue keeping us stuck. You can think of it like a dandelion growing in the middle of your well-manicured lawn. The content issue is that bright yellow flower. It is blatant, apparent, and easy to get rid of. Just pluck that dandelion head right off and suddenly your lawn is once again an unrelenting expanse of greenness. But . . . you know what happens next. The dandelion blooms again, and probably multiplies at the same time. Why? Because you didn't address the roots.

The pattern-, process-, and relationship-level issues in our lives are like those roots. Until we identify and address them, we will face the same content issues again and again.

But beware. Just because you know you need to have a pattern- or relationship-level conversation doesn't make it easy. Once you have chosen the level of the conversation, it is up to you to keep it there. More often than not, when you step up to a pattern- or relationship-level conversation with someone, the other person's tendency will be to seek safety in a content-level conversation.

For example, you've noticed over the last several months that the creative output of one of your designers seems to be a bit stale. He's hitting all his deadlines and producing the requested deliverables. But the quality and innovation just aren't where you want them to be. It's not a problem of any one specific design. Rather, when taken as a body of work, his recent output isn't up to the same standards as it used to be. You decide to step up to this pattern conversation.

"Have a look," you say. "Here are the last five designs you've produced, and here are the five before that. As I see it, those from the past six months aren't at the same level of creativity as your previous work. Technically, they are right on target. But creatively, they have lost some shine. I'm interested in how you see it."

He quickly responds, "I know my work on the Johnson project this week wasn't as good as it could have been. It was really confusing to know what the client wanted, and I was balancing a ton of other projects at the same time."

Do you see what just happened there? You stepped up to a pattern conversation (the last six months of designs), and he responded by talking about a content issue (the very last design he did). Now, at this point, it can be very easy to get sucked into that conversation. It's as easy as saying, "Yes, I know there is a lot going on, but the Johnson project was really critical for us as a team. We needed your best work." And just like that, you're holding a different conversation than the one you intended. You'll walk away feeling unresolved. Why? Because you held the wrong conversation.

There is no malintent here on the part of the graphic designer. He isn't purposely trying to steer you off course. He's just fallen into the trap we all fall into . . . choosing recent over right, or easy over hard. It's up to you to keep the conversation at the level you want it by saying, "I know there was a lot going on this week along with the Johnson project. I get that. And I'm actually less concerned with the specifics of the Johnson project than I am with the pattern I'm seeing in your work over the last six months. I'm wondering if there's something bigger going on here that's keeping you from delivering your best work."

Generally, you should choose the level at which you want to hold the conversation and then keep it there. However, there is an exception.

Place a Bookmark

Clarity is crucial. But so is flexibility. Remember, this isn't a monologue. It should be a dialogue. There are other people in this conversation, and they have their own wants and needs. In some Crucial Conversations, new issues will come up, and you need to balance focus (on your goals) with flexibility (to meet their goals).

Let's listen in as Tyra talks to her coworker Katy about some data she needs:

> **Tyra:** *I was expecting to get the raw data file for Project Ascent yesterday, but I haven't seen it yet. Is the file ready?*
>
> **Katy:** *The system's down this morning. I am totally locked out. I swear, I don't know how we're supposed to do our jobs around here if they can't even keep the systems running, right?*
>
> **Tyra:** *Well, maybe, but was the system down yesterday?*
>
> **Katy:** *Hey, who died and left you in charge? Why are you all over me on this? We're friends. Can't you cut me a little slack?*
>
> **Tyra:** *We are friends. And coworkers. I'm not trying to hound you. I just need this report.*
>
> **Katy:** *I know, I know. Sorry. I guess I'm just all uptight because I already had to deal with Mark today, and eew! That guy just gives me the creeps. I can't handle the way his eyes crawl all over me. I am just on edge. Sorry.*

Well, that was a lot more than Tyra bargained for. She started to address what seemed like a pretty straightforward issue, the missing data file, and she got three issues right back: the system is down; the "aren't we friends" manipulation; and, most concerning, an implication of harassment.

What do you do when you start a conversation focused on one issue and new issues emerge? You have a choice to make. You can either stay focused on the original issue or move to a new one. In all cases, you want to place a bookmark. When you place a bookmark, you verbally acknowledge where you're going in the conversation and what you intend to come back to.

Let's say Tyra wants to move to this new issue, her friend's experience with Mark. She moves to the new issue and bookmarks the original issue by saying:

> **Tyra:** *Wow! I can tell you're upset. Let's talk about this. We'll come back to the data file later.*

In some cases, although probably not this one given the seriousness of the emergent issue, you may want to bookmark the new issue and stay focused on the original:

> **Tyra:** *Wow! That's a big deal, and I really want to talk to you about what you are experiencing because it needs to be addressed. At the same time, I have 30 minutes to get this data file over to the ops team. Let's figure out this data file issue and then come back to Mark. Because that needs to be addressed.*

When you place a bookmark, you make a conscious choice about what you want to talk about. And you register clearly with the other person that you will return to the bookmarked issue later. Never allow the conversation to shift or the topic to change without acknowledging you've done it.

BACK TO WENDY

Remember Wendy? She was facing a pretty complex conversation with her manager. They started out talking about a project timeline. As the conversation progressed, new issues came into play. How decisions were being made. What input was being considered. And the pressure that Sandrine was putting on Wendy with veiled threats. Let's see how Wendy responded.

When Sandrine said, "Look, I really pushed for you to be the one to lead this project. Do you know what I said about you? I said you were a team player. Was I mistaken?," Wendy made the smart choice in this situation to bookmark the project timeline (the content issue) and move the conversation to the relationship level. Her simple problem sentence was "This is about whether I can trust our process and trust you."

She responded to Sandrine, saying, "I get we're in a tough spot here. I don't want to disappoint our leadership any more than you do. And I want you to know that I'm committed to getting stuff done. At the same time, I want us to set realistic goals; otherwise, we're setting ourselves up to fail. And maybe even more important, I want us to work together in a way where we're up front with each other about our needs and concerns."

This was the start of a relationship conversation. And the start of a better relationship.

SUMMARY: CHOOSE YOUR TOPIC

You can't solve the real problem if you don't choose the right topic. Here's how to make sure you are talking about the right thing:

- Learn the three signs you're having the wrong conversation:

  1. Your emotions escalate.
  2. You walk away skeptical.

3. You're in a déjà vu dialogue.

- Use three skills to identify your topic, and prepare to keep focused on it:

    1. **Unbundle.** Unpack the various issues at play using CPR. Are they content, pattern, or relationship concerns or perhaps process?
    2. **Choose.** Ask yourself: "What do I really want?" Use this as a filter to choose which topic is most relevant at the moment.
    3. **Simplify.** Condense your concern into a single sentence so you can maintain focus once the conversation gets under way.

- Finally, be both focused and flexible. Pay attention to others' unintentional, or intentional, efforts to change the topic. Don't allow the topic to change without a conscious decision. And if you do decide to shift topics, bookmark the original one to make it easy to return to after the new topic is handled.

4

START WITH HEART

How to Stay Focused on What You Really Want

Now that you know what you want to talk about, it's time to turn to the *how* of dialogue. How do you encourage the flow of meaning when you're in the thrall of strong emotions talking about things that matter deeply to you with those who disagree vehemently? Given that most people's style is based on longstanding habits, it'll probably require a lot of effort.

The truth is, people *can* change. In fact, we've taught these conversation skills to millions around the world and have seen dramatic improvements in results and relationships. But it requires work. You can't simply highlight an inspiring paragraph in a book and walk away changed. Instead, you'll need to start by taking a long, hard look at yourself.

That's why Start with Heart is the foundation of dialogue. Change begins with *your* heart. Our bias is the opposite. Our bodies are designed to gather data about others, not ourselves. To paraphrase Shakespeare, the eye sees everything but itself. We can hear how others are overstating their points. We can see how they're clenching their fists and spraying spittle while they harangue us. What we fail to notice is our own eye roll, head shake, and sneer.

One of the most important lessons we've learned from those who do their best during crucial moments is that it all begins with *me*. The first thing that degenerates during a Crucial Conversation is not your behavior; it's your motive. And we can rarely see it happening. The first step to dialogue is to get your heart right.

WORK ON ME *FIRST*, US SECOND

Let's start with a true story. Two young sisters, Aislinn and Cara, and their father scurry into their hotel room after spending a hot afternoon at Disneyland. Given the repressive heat, the girls have consumed enough soda to irrigate a small farm. As the two bursting kids enter their room, they have but one thought—to head for the head.

Since the bathroom is a one-holer, it isn't long until a fight breaks out. The desperate children start arguing, pushing, and name-calling as they dance around the tiny bathroom. Eventually Aislinn calls out to her father for help.

"Dad, I got here first!"

"I know, but I need to go worse!" says Cara.

"How do you know? You're not in my body. I didn't even go before we left this morning!"

"You're so selfish."

Dad, in a naïve attempt to teach them to solve their own problems, proposes a plan: "Girls, I'm not going to solve this for you. You can stay in the bathroom and figure out who goes first and who goes second. There's only one rule. No hitting."

As the two antsy kids begin their Crucial Conversation, Dad checks his watch. He wonders how long it'll take. As the minutes slowly tick away, he hears nothing more than an occasional outburst of sarcasm. Finally after 25 long minutes, the toilet flushes. Cara comes out. A minute later, another flush and out walks Aislinn. With both girls in the room, Dad asks, "Do you know how many times both of you could have gone to the bathroom in the time it took you to work that out?"

The idea had not occurred to the little scamps. Dad then probes further: "Why did it take so long for the two of you to use the bathroom?"

"Because she's always so selfish!"

"Listen to her. She's calling *me* names when *she* could have just waited. She always has to have her way!"

Both girls claimed what they wanted most was to go to the bathroom. Then they behaved in ways that ensured the bathroom was little more than a distant dream. Based on the 25-minute bathroom dance, what was their *real* motive? To experience the blessed relief of using the toilet? No. Sometimes the best way to discern motive is to examine behavior. By looking at how the sisters were acting, we can see what they *really* wanted was to be first, to be right, or perhaps even to make the other sister miserable.

The first problem we face in our Crucial Conversations is not that our behavior degenerates. It's that our motives do—a shift that we are often completely unaware of. Instead, we cling to our "stated" motive and ignore what our behavior reveals about our true motive.

The first step in achieving the results we *really* want is to stop believing that others are the source of all that ails us. Our sister is not the problem; our motives are. It's our dogmatic conviction that "if we could just fix those losers, all would go better" that keeps us from taking action that could lead to dialogue and progress. It's no surprise then that those who are *best* at dialogue tend to turn this logic around. They believe the best way to work on "us" is to start with "me."

People who are *best* at dialogue understand this simple fact and turn it into the principle "Work on me first, us second." They realize not only that they are likely to benefit by improving their own approach, but also that the only ones they can work on anyway are themselves. As much as others may need to change, or we may *want* them to change, the only person we can continually inspire, prod, and shape—with any degree of success—is the person in the mirror.

START WITH HEART

OK, let's assume we need to work on our own personal dialogue skills. Instead of buying this book and handing it to a loved one or coworker and saying, "You'll love this, especially the parts that I've underlined for you," we'll try to figure out how we ourselves can benefit. But where do we start?

Skilled people Start with Heart. That is, they begin high-risk discussions with the right motives, and they stay focused on those motives no matter what happens.

They maintain this focus in two ways. First, they're steely-eyed smart when it comes to knowing what they want. Despite constant impulses to slip away from their goals, they stick with them. Second, skilled people don't make Fool's Choices. Unlike others who justify their unhealthy behavior by explaining that they had no choice but to fight or take flight, the dialogue-smart believe that dialogue, no matter the circumstances, is always an option.

A Moment of Truth

Let's look at a real-life example of how losing sight of our motives can affect our ability to stay in dialogue.

Greta, the CEO of a midsized corporation, is two hours into a rather tense meeting with her top leaders. For the past six months, she has been on a personal campaign to reduce costs. Little has been accomplished to date, so Greta calls the meeting. Surely people will tell her why they haven't started cutting costs. After all, she has taken great pains to foster candor.

Greta has just opened the meeting to questions when a manager haltingly rises to his feet, fidgets, stares at the floor, and then nervously asks if he can ask a very tough question. The way the fellow emphasizes the word "very" makes it sound as if he's about to accuse Greta of perpetrating 9/11.

The frightened manager continues: "Greta, you've been asking us for six months to find ways to cut costs. I'd be lying if I said that we've given you much more than a lukewarm response. If you don't mind, I'd like to tell you about one thing that's making it tough for us to take this seriously."

"Great. Fire away," Greta says as she smiles in response. This is exactly what she wants—to hear what the barriers are so that she can address them and let the cost cutting begin.

"Well, while you've been asking us to use both sides of our paper and forgo travel, you're having a second office built."

Greta freezes and turns bright red. Everyone looks to see what will happen next.

The manager plunges on ahead: "The rumor is that the furniture alone will cost hundreds of thousands of dollars. Is that right?"

The conversation has just turned crucial. Someone has just poured a radioactive liquid into the pool of meaning. Will Greta continue to encourage honest feedback, or will she shut the fellow down?

How Greta acts during the next few moments not only will set people's attitudes toward the proposed cost-cutting initiative, but will also have a huge impact on what the other leaders think about her. Does she walk the talk of openness and honesty? Or is she a raging hypocrite—like so many of the senior executives who came before her?

What Is She Acting Like She Wants?

As we watch Greta, something quite subtle and yet very important takes place. Greta's jaw tightens. She leans forward and grips the left side of the rostrum hard enough that her knuckles turn white. She lifts her right hand, with the finger pointing at the questioner like a loaded weapon. She hasn't said anything yet, but it is clear where Greta is heading. She has been attacked publicly, and she is preparing to defend herself. In less time than it takes her to clear her thoughts, her motive has changed from succeeding with cost cutting to something less noble.

What Greta cares most about right now is not getting results, but getting revenge. She isn't worried about how the company performs; she's worried about how she appears. When under attack, our hearts can take a similarly sudden and unconscious turn. When faced with pressure and strong opinions, we often stop worrying about the goal of adding to the pool of meaning and start looking for ways to win, save face, keep the peace, or punish others. Just ask Greta. "To heck with honest communication!" she thinks to herself. "I'll teach the moron not to attack me in public."

"Is that a *serious* question?" she wants to ask. She wants to say, "If we want to win bigger customers, we need a facility that shows some self-confidence. If you had an executive mindset, you'd understand this. Next question."

At the sight of her pointing her finger, everyone immediately clammed up and looked at the floor. The silence was deafening, for a moment, as everyone waited for what came next.

FIRST, FOCUS ON WHAT YOU REALLY WANT

Then Greta did something remarkable. Almost as soon as her finger rose like a loaded pistol, it dropped back to her side. Her face relaxed. At first she looked surprised, embarrassed, and maybe even a little upset. But then she took a deep breath and said: "You know what? We need to talk about this. I'm glad you asked the question. Thank you for taking that risk. I appreciate the trust it shows in me."

Wow! In a matter of seconds she had transformed from a danger-ous weapon into a curious partner.

And then Greta got real. She acknowledged the apparent hypoc-risy in talking cost cutting while spending on a new office. She admitted that she did not know what the project would cost and asked someone to leave the meeting to check the numbers. She explained that building the office was a response to marketing's advice to boost the company's image and improve client confidence. And while Greta *would* use the office, it would be primarily a hosting location for marketing. "But," she added, "I have not managed this project as tightly as I'm asking you to manage yours. And that's hypocritical." When she saw the figures for the office, Greta was stunned and admitted that she should have checked the costs before signing a work order.

A wonderfully candid exchange followed wherein various partic-ipants in the meeting expressed their views about the propriety of the project. In the end, they agreed to move ahead, but cut the costs by half or cancel the project entirely. Widespread support for cost cutting took off from that moment.

As we watched this interaction, we wondered what had hap-pened to Greta. How did she remain so composed while under fire? Specifically, how did she move so quickly from wanting to humiliate the questioner to sincerely soliciting feedback?

Later that day we asked Greta about that transformation. We wanted to know exactly what had been going on in her head. What had helped her move from embarrassment and anger to gratitude?

"It was easy," Greta explained. "At first I did feel attacked, and I wanted to strike back. To be honest, I wanted to put that guy in his place. He was accusing me in public, and he was wrong."

"But," she continued, "I've learned that when my emotions take over, the best way to get back into control is to focus on a simple question."

At this point she had our full attention. Could asking your-self a single question truly transform your emotions the way we had witnessed it happening with Greta? And if so, what question should you ask?

She continued, "When I feel threatened, I pause, take a breath, and ask, 'What do I *really* want?'"

"Really?" we asked. "And how did that help?"

"The first answer that came up for me was, 'I want to humiliate this guy who is attacking me!' That was my emotions talking. So I pressed again, 'What do I *really* want?' And that's when the clarity came: 'What I really want is for 200 managers to leave here supportive of cost cutting.'"

Greta went on: "When that commitment settled inside me, it transformed the way I saw the man in the back of the room. Whereas seconds earlier he looked like an enemy, when my motive changed I could see he was the best ally I had in the room. He was the one handing me the best chance I had of dealing with the resistance I was facing. It was easy then to respond in the right way."

Suddenly Greta's rapid transformation from tyrant to leader made sense. When her motive changed from saving face to solving a problem, it was perfectly natural for her first words to be: "You know what? We need to talk about this. I'm glad you asked the question. Thank you for taking that risk."

Greta taught us that a small, mental intervention—the simple act of asking a potent question—can have a powerful effect on redirecting our hearts.

Refocus Your Brain

Now let's move to a situation you might face. You're speaking with someone who completely disagrees with you on a hot issue. How does all this motive stuff apply? As you begin the discussion, start by examining your motives. Going in, ask yourself what you really want.

As the conversation unfolds and you find yourself starting to, say, defer to the boss or give your partner the cold shoulder, pay attention to what's happening to your objectives. Are you starting to worry more about saving face, avoiding embarrassment, winning, being right, or punishing others? Here's the tricky part. Our motives usually change without any conscious thought on our part. When adrenaline does our thinking for us, our motives flow with the chemical tide. In a sense, you don't choose the motive; it chooses you. But if you can see it, you can change it.

The first step to getting back to a healthy motive is to become aware of the one that's possessing you. This is harder than it might seem. In our adrenaline-drunk, dumbed-down state, we're often not very skillful at subtle self-awareness. So what's a human to do?

Look for clues. Discern your motives from the outside in. In order to move back to motives that allow for dialogue, you must step away from the interaction and look at yourself—much like an outsider would. Ask yourself, "What am I *acting* like I want?" Take a look at your behavior, and work backward to the motive. As you make an honest effort to discover your motive, you might conclude: "Let's see. I'm cutting people off, overstating my points, and shaking my head every time they talk. Aha! I've shifted from planning a great vacation to winning an argument."

Once you humbly acknowledge the shifting desires of your heart, you can make conscious choices to change them. The fastest way to free yourself of a hurtful motive is to simply admit you've got it. When you name the game, you can stop playing it.

Now ask, "What do I *really* want?" Ask yourself these three questions:

"What do I really want for myself?"

"What do I really want for others?"

"What do I really want for the relationship?"

Once you're free of the lower motive, healthy answers will come quickly and easily: "What I really want is for us to all feel great about the vacation spot we choose."

Once you've asked yourself what you want, add one more equally telling question:

"What should I do right now to move toward what I really want?"

Taken together, these four questions are a powerful tool for refocusing your brain. Here's how:

Play the long game. These questions form powerful emotional interventions when we need it most. You can't rush through them. If you do, you'll end up answering them insincerely and with a short-term focus. You may have to ask them each several times before you can dig down deep enough to reconnect with a long-term motive.

Years ago, we watched this play out with a young brother and sister who were racing across a grassy field. When they got to the edge of the field, the sister turned to her brother and triumphantly cried, "I win! I win!" Then, after no more than a heartbeat, added, "You lose! You lose!" What did she want for herself in that moment? To win. What did she want for her brother? To lose. When we are caught in the passion of the moment and our motives have shifted, we become myopic, focusing on what we really want . . . right now. To move out of that near-term focus, you may need to ask yourself these questions more than once.

You may also find it helpful to add "long term" to the questions. Asking "What do I really want for myself in the long term?" helps us shift our focus from our immediate, near-term desires to a more profound consideration of who we want to be: "What kind of person do I want to be?" "How do I want to treat others?" "How do I need to show up in this conversation in order to be that kind of person?"

Reengage Your Brain

These questions are also a powerful tool for reengaging your brain. The reason they are so potent is that they help massage the higher reasoning centers of your brain back into activity, calming the fight-or-flight instinct. It works this way: When you pose complex and abstract questions to yourself, the problem-solving part of your brain recognizes that you are now dealing with intricate social issues and not physical threats. When we present our brain with a demanding question, our body sends blood to the parts of our brain that help us think and away from the parts of our body that help us take flight or begin a fight.

SECOND, REFUSE THE FOOL'S CHOICE

Now let's add one more tool that helps us focus on what we really want. We'll start with a story.

Tally is scrolling through her social media feed when she stumbles on a passionate debate about a proposed curriculum change for her kids' school. Wanting to be an informed parent, she carefully reads the lengthy post and the numerous comments that follow. The discussion is robust, and parents both for and against the proposed changes are making reasonable arguments. Tally finds herself agreeing with people on both sides of the argument.

Then Gloria, who lives in the building across the street, starts to weigh in. Gloria expresses her loathing for the proposed changes with strong language and ALL CAPS!!!!! She knows, without a shadow of a doubt, that these curriculum changes will ruin all the neighborhood kids, all of whom will end up dropping out of school and selling drugs as a result.

Predictably, people begin to push back on Gloria. Gloria responds by pushing back on the pushback. Soon the debate is no longer about curriculum; it's about the idiots who dare to think differently than she does. As Tally reads on, she feels her blood start to boil. These are her neighbors and friends that Gloria is attacking! This isn't right. Someone needs to put Gloria in her place and stop these vicious posts.

Tally's fingers fly as she taps out a response to Gloria's latest post: "@Gloria—you are the one who is an idiot. Principal Johnson has turned this school around. If she says this curriculum is the way to help our kids, then it is. You have no qualifications or standing here. You didn't even graduate from high school. You are a big phony when it comes to education, and I am not going to stand by and let you attack people who are actually qualified to discuss the education of our children!"

Tally stabs her finger at the screen, posting her message with a feeling of righteousness. Someone had to stand up to Gloria. Within moments, Tally hears the ding of an incoming direct message. It's from another neighbor, Miguel. "Whoa, Tally, that was a little harsh, don't you think?" Then another from Sandra. And Karyn. And Tyrone. It's clear that Tally's fellow parents are taken aback by her takedown of Gloria.

Tally utters, and then messages, the words we've all come to hate: "Hey, don't look at me like that! I'm the only one around who has the guts to speak the truth."

What a tactic. Tally attacks Gloria in public, and then instead of apologizing or maybe simply fading into the shadows, she argues that what she just did was somehow noble.

She's just made the Fool's Choice. Her statement assumes she had to choose between telling the truth and keeping a friend.

Those who are skilled at Crucial Conversations present their brains with a more complex question. They ask, "What do I want for myself, the other person, *and* the relationship?"

As you practice presenting this question to yourself at emotional times, you'll discover that at first you resist it. When our brain isn't functioning well, we resist complexity. It seems, well, complex! We adore the ease of simply choosing between attacking or hiding—and the fact that we think it makes us look good: "I'm sorry, but I just had to destroy her self-image if I was going to keep my integrity. It wasn't pretty, but it was the right thing to do."

Fortunately, when you refuse the Fool's Choice and instead require your brain to solve the more complex problem, more often than not, your brain does just that. You'll find there is a way to share your concerns, listen sincerely to those of others, and build the relationship—all at the same time. And the results can be life changing.

Search for the Elusive "And"

The *best* at dialogue refuse Fool's Choices by setting up new choices. They present themselves with tougher questions that turn the either/or choice into a search for the all-important and ever-elusive "and." (It is an endangered species, you know.) Here's how this works:

First, clarify what you *really* want. You've got a head start if you've already Started with Heart. If you know what you want for yourself, for others, and for the relationship, then you're in position to break out of the Fool's Choice:

> "What I want is to engage in community discussion about
> a curriculum that impacts all our kids. I want our group
> of parents to be able to share candidly and listen to one
> another."

Second, clarify what you really *don't* want. This is the key to framing the *and* question. Think of what you are afraid will happen to you if you back away from your current strategy of trying to win or stay safe. What bad thing will happen if you stop pushing so hard? Or if you don't try to escape? What horrible outcome makes game playing an attractive and sensible option?

"What I don't want is to have people shut down because one person is dominating the discussion thread and throwing insults. I also don't want our honest difference to lead to damaged relationships."

Third, present your brain with a more complex problem. Finally, combine the two into an *and* question that forces you to search for more creative and productive options than silence or violence:

"How can we have a candid conversation and strengthen our relationships?"

It's interesting to watch what happens when people are presented with *and* questions after being stuck with Fool's Choices. Their faces become reflective, their eyes open wider, and they begin to *think*. With surprising regularity, when people are asked, "Is it possible that there's a way to accomplish both?" they acknowledge that there very well may be:

"Is there a way to tell your peer your real concerns and not insult or offend him?"

"Is there a way to talk to your neighbors about their annoying behavior and not come across as self-righteous or demanding?"

"Is there a way to talk with your loved one about how you're spending money and not get into an argument?"

Is This Really Possible?

Some people believe that this whole line of thinking is comically unrealistic. From their point of view, Fool's Choices aren't false dichotomies; they're merely a reflection of an unfortunate reality. For example: "You can't say something to the boss about our upcoming move. It'll cost you your job."

To these people we say, remember Kevin? He, and almost every other opinion leader we've ever studied, has what it takes to speak up *and* maintain respect. Maybe you don't know what Kevin did or what you need to do—but don't deny the existence of Kevin or people like him. There is a third set of options out there that allows you to add meaning to the pool *and* build on the relationship.

When we (the authors) are in the middle of an on-site workshop and we suggest there are alternatives to Fool's Choices, someone invariably says, "Maybe you can speak honestly and still be heard in other organizations, but if you try it here, you'll be eaten alive!" Or the flip side, "You've got to know when to fold if you want to survive for another day."

At first, we thought that maybe there *were* places where dialogue couldn't survive. But then we learned to ask, "Are you saying there isn't *anyone* you know who is able to hold a high-risk conversation in a way that solves problems *and* builds relationships?" There usually is.

SUMMARY: START WITH HEART

Here's how people who are skilled at dialogue stay focused on their goals—particularly when the going gets tough.

Work on *Me* First, Us Second

- Remember that the only person you can directly control is yourself.

Focus on What You Really Want

- When you find yourself moving toward silence or violence, stop and pay attention to your motives.
- Ask yourself: "What am I acting like I want?"
- Then, clarify what you *really* want. Ask yourself: "What do I want for myself? For others? For the relationship?"
- And finally, ask: "What should I do right now to move toward what I really want?"

Refuse the Fool's Choice

- As you consider what you want, notice when you start talking yourself into a Fool's Choice.
- Break free of these Fool's Choices by searching for the "and."
- Clarify what you don't want, add it to what you do want, and ask your brain to start searching for healthy options to bring you to dialogue.

5

MASTER MY STORIES

How to Stay in Dialogue When
You're Angry, Scared, or Hurt

Here's where we are in our Crucial Conversation:

- We've recognized the conversation might be crucial (Chapters 1 and 2).
- We've even zeroed in on the right conversation to address (Chapter 3).
- We've thought about what we really want (Chapter 4).

We are almost ready to open our mouths. But not quite yet. We still have one problem to solve: We don't *feel* like engaging in dialogue. What we *feel* like doing would forever eliminate the chance to run for public office.

As we learned in Chapter 2, one of the defining features of Crucial Conversations is strong emotions. Without these emotions, most of us do just fine in a conversation. We can talk about the weather like a champ. But when our emotions come into play, we often become the very worst version of ourselves, and the conversation nosedives. This

73

chapter explores how to gain control of Crucial Conversations by learning how to take charge of your emotions. How you respond to your own emotions is the best predictor of everything that matters in life. It is the very essence of emotional intelligence. By learning to exert influence over your own feelings, you'll place yourself in a far better position to use all the tools of Crucial Conversations.

HE MADE ME MAD!

How many times have you heard someone say, "He made me mad!"? How many times have you said it? For instance, you're sitting quietly at home watching TV, and your mother-in-law (who lives with you) walks in. She glances around and then starts picking up the mess you made a few minutes earlier when you whipped up a batch of nachos. This ticks you off. She's always smugly skulking around the house, thinking you're a slob.

A few minutes later when your spouse asks you why you're so upset, you explain: "It's your mom again. I was lying here enjoying myself when she gave me that look. To be honest, I wish she would quit doing that. It's my only day off, I'm relaxing quietly, and then she walks in and starts judging me. It drives me nuts."

"Does *she* drive you nuts?" your spouse asks. "Or do you?"

That's an interesting question.

No matter who is doing the driving, some people tend to react more explosively than others—and to the same stimulus, no less. Why is that? For instance, what enables some people to listen to withering feedback without flinching, whereas others pitch a fit when you tell them they've got a smear of salsa on their chin? Why is it that sometimes you yourself can take a verbal blow to the gut without batting an eye, but other times you go ballistic if someone so much as looks at you sideways?

EMOTIONS DON'T JUST HAPPEN

To answer these questions, we'll start with two rather bold (and sometimes unpopular) claims. Then we'll explain the logic behind each claim.

Claim one. Emotions don't settle upon you like a fog. They are not foisted upon you by others. No matter how comfortable it might make you feel to say it, others don't make you mad. *You* make you mad. You make you scared, annoyed, insulted, or hurt. You and only you create your emotions.

Claim two. Once you've created your upset emotions, you have only two options: You can act on them or be acted on by them. That is, when it comes to strong emotions, you either find a way to master them or fall hostage to them.

Here's how this all unfolds:

Maria's Story

Consider Maria, a copywriter who is currently being held hostage to some pretty strong emotions. She and her colleague Louis just reviewed the latest draft of a proposal with their boss. During the meeting, they were supposed to be jointly presenting their ideas. But when Maria paused to take a breath, Louis took over the presentation, making almost all the points they had come up with together. When the boss turned to Maria for input, there was nothing left for her to say.

Maria has been feeling humiliated and angry throughout this project. First, Louis took their suggestions to the boss and discussed them behind her back. And now he completely monopolized the presentation.

Maria believes Louis is downplaying her contribution because she's the only woman on the team.

She's getting fed up with his "boys' club" mentality. So what does she do? She doesn't want to appear "oversensitive," so most of the time she says nothing and just does her job. However, she does manage to assert herself by occasionally getting in sarcastic jabs about the way she's being treated.

"Sure I can get that printout for you. Should I just get your coffee and whip up a bundt cake while I'm at it?" she mutters, and she rolls her eyes as she exits the room.

Louis, in turn, finds Maria's cheap shots and sarcasm puzzling. He's not sure what has Maria upset but is beginning to resent her hostile reaction to almost everything he does. As a result, when the two work together, you could cut the tension with a knife.

What's Making Maria (and Louis) Mad?

The *worst* at dialogue fall into the trap Maria has fallen into. Maria is completely unaware of a dangerous assumption she's making. She's upset at being overlooked and is keeping a "professional silence." She's assuming that her emotions and behavior are the only right and reasonable reactions under the circumstances. She's convinced that anyone in her place would feel the same way.

Here's the problem. Maria is treating her emotions as if they are the only valid response. Since, in her mind, they are both justified and accurate, she makes no effort to change or even question them. Besides, in her view, Louis caused them. Ultimately, her actions (saying nothing and taking cheap shots) are being driven by these very emotions. Her emotions are controlling her behavior and fueling her deteriorating relationship with Louis. The *worst* at dialogue fall hostage to their emotions, and they don't even know it.

The *good* at dialogue realize that if they don't control their emotions, matters will get worse. So they try something else. They fake it. They take a deep breath and count to 10. They choke down reactions and then do their best to get back to dialogue. At least, they give it a shot.

Unfortunately, once these emotionally choked folks hit a rough spot in a Crucial Conversation, their suppressed emotions come out of hiding. These suppressed emotions show up as tightened jaws or sarcastic comments. Dialogue dies. Or maybe people's paralyzing fear causes them to avoid saying what they really think. Meaning is kept out of the pool because it's cut off at the source. In any case, their emotions sneak out of the cubbyhole they've been crammed into and find a way to creep into the conversation. It's never pretty, and it always kills dialogue.

The *best* at dialogue do something completely different. They aren't held hostage by their emotions, nor do they try to hide or suppress them. Instead, they act *on* their emotions. That is, when they have strong feelings, they influence (and often change) their emotions by *thinking them out*. As a result, they choose their emotions, and by so doing, make it possible to choose behaviors that create better results.

This, of course, is easier said than done. It's not easy to *rethink* yourself from an emotional and dangerous state into one that puts you back in control. But it can be done. It should be done.

THE PATH TO ACTION

To help rethink our emotions, we need to know where our feelings come from in the first place. Let's look at a model that helps us examine and then gain control of our own emotions.

Consider Maria. She's feeling hurt but is worried that if she says something to Louis, she'll look too emotional. So she alternates between holding her feelings inside and taking cheap shots.

As Figure 5.1 demonstrates, Maria's actions stem from her feelings. First she feels, and then she acts. That's easy enough, but it prompts the question: What's causing Maria's feelings in the first place?

Is it Louis's behavior? As was the case with the nacho–mother-in-law incident, did Louis *make* Maria feel insulted and hurt? Maria heard and saw Louis jump in and deliver several key points in their presentation that she was planning to cover. Based on what she saw and heard, she generated an emotion, and then she acted out her feelings.

Figure 5.1

So here's the big question: What happens between what Maria sees and hears (i.e., Louis acting) and what she feels? Does what we see, hear, or experience make us feel something (see Figure 5.2)? And if so, why do different people feel differently under the same circumstances?

Figure 5.2

Stories Create Feelings

As it turns out, there is an intermediate step between what others do and how we feel. Just *after* we observe what others do and just *before* we feel some emotion about it, we tell ourselves a story. We add meaning to the action we observed. We make a guess at the motive driving the behavior. Why were they doing that? We also add judgment—is that good or bad? And then, based on these thoughts or stories, our body responds with an emotion.

This intermediate step is why, when faced with the exact same circumstances, 10 people may have 10 different emotional responses. For instance, with a coworker like Louis, some might feel insulted, whereas others merely feel curious. Some become angry, and others feel concern or even sympathy.

Pictorially it looks like the model in Figure 5.3. We call this model our Path to Action because it explains how experiences, thoughts, and feelings lead to our actions.

You'll note that we've added telling a story to our model. We observe, *we tell a story*, and then we feel. Although this addition complicates the model a bit, it also gives us hope. Since we *and only we* are telling the story, we can take back control of our own emotions by telling a different story. We now have a point of leverage or control. If we can find a way to change the stories we tell by rethinking or retelling them, we can master our emotions and, therefore, master our Crucial Conversations.

Figure 5.3 Path to Action

OUR STORIES

Nothing in this world is good or bad, but thinking makes it so.

—WILLIAM SHAKESPEARE

Stories provide our rationale for what's going on. They're our interpretations of the facts. They start by helping to explain what we see and hear ("Carl is walking out of the building with a bright yellow box. Yellow boxes contain secure material"). But usually stories take the *what* a step further and give voice to *why* something is happening ("Carl is stealing our intellectual property"). Our stories contain not just conclusions but also judgments (whether something is good or bad) and attributions (interpretation of others' motives).

Think about Maria and Louis. Maria observes that Louis has started talking and now won't stop. What is happening here? Maria concludes that Louis is *taking over the presentation*. But Maria's story doesn't stop there. She quickly tells herself a story about *why* Louis is taking over the presentation: "He doesn't trust my ability to communicate. He thinks that they're more likely to listen to a man. And he's trying to hog the spotlight for himself." She begins to attribute motive to Louis's actions, and then she makes a judgment: "He's a sexist, power-hungry weasel."

Of course, as we come up with our own meaning or stories, it isn't long until our body responds with strong feelings or emotions—after all, our emotions are directly linked to our judgments of right/wrong, good/bad, kind/selfish, fair/unfair, etc. Maria's story yields anger and frustration. These feelings, in turn, drive Maria to her actions—toggling back and forth between clamming up and taking an occasional cheap shot (see Figure 5.4).

Figure 5.4 Maria's Path to Action

A Few Facts About Stories

Even if you don't realize it, you are telling yourself stories. When we teach people that it's our stories that drive our emotions and not other people's actions, someone inevitably raises a hand and says: "Wait a minute! I didn't notice myself telling a story. When that guy laughed at me during my presentation, I just *felt* angry. The feelings came first; the thoughts came second." Storytelling typically happens blindingly fast. When we believe we're at risk, we tell ourselves a story so quickly that we don't even know we're doing it. If you don't believe this is true, ask yourself whether you *always* become angry when someone laughs at you. If sometimes you do and sometimes you don't, then your response *isn't* hardwired. That means something goes on between *others laughing* and *you feeling*. In truth, you tell a story. You may not remember it, but you tell a story.

Any set of facts can be used to tell an infinite number of stories. Stories are just that—stories. These explanations could be told in numerous different ways. For instance, Maria could just as easily have decided that Louis didn't realize she cared so much about the project. She could have concluded that Louis was feeling unimportant and this was a way of showing he was valuable. Or maybe he had been burned in the past because he hadn't personally seen through every detail of a project. Any of these stories would have fit the facts and would have created very different emotions.

If we take control of our stories, they won't control us. People who excel at dialogue are able to influence their emotions during Crucial Conversations. They recognize that while it's true that at first we are in control of the stories we tell, once they're told, *the stories control us.* They first control how we feel and then how we act. And thus they control the results we get from our Crucial Conversations.

———

The good news is we can tell different stories and break the loop. In fact, *until* we tell different stories, we *cannot* break the loop.

If you want improved results from your Crucial Conversations, change the stories you tell yourself—even while you're in the middle of the fray.

WHY MASTER OUR STORIES?

We're about to share some very effective tools you can use to expose, examine, and improve your story. We confess up front that these skills take work. They take focus, concentration, and humility. Many readers make it halfway through this section and shout at the book something akin to, "Why do I have to do all this #^&(@ work?!" Translated, they're asking, "Why not live the simple life of blaming others for causing our emotions?"

The truth is, you don't have to do this work. Unless you want different results. If you want different results, you'll need different emotions. If Maria wants to get different results and have a different working relationship with Louis, she is going to have to act in different ways. In order to act differently, she'll need to feel differently. In order to feel differently, she must master her story.

Mastering our stories isn't about letting someone off the hook for bad behavior. Instead, it is the first step toward addressing that behavior through dialogue. When we master our stories, we take ownership for the emotional energy we bring to the conversation. And when we do that, we begin to change the conversation.

Another reason it's risky to leave your story unexamined is that your story might be creating your reality. Most often, when people defend their story, they are saying that their story is an accurate reflection of reality. The reality came first, and their story merely captured it. Maybe. But when you dig deeper, it is not uncommon to find that the story itself created the reality. Or at least contributed to it. We call this a "downward spiral." Here is a real-life example of how it works. It happened to Joseph early in his marriage. He describes it this way:

I'd been married for just a few years; a couple of children had come along, and my travel schedule was starting to become hectic. Celia, my wife, agreed to be the sole parent when I was gone. I came home from a trip one evening. Celia was sitting on the couch reading. I was about to say hello when the phone rang. I had two immediate thoughts: (1) Answer the phone; it could be an international emergency that only I can solve. (2) Don't answer the phone! The love of my life would like time with me.

I had a clear feeling about what I should do. But I violated it. I picked up the phone. It was one of my business partners, and I began a conversation.

Now, stay with me here because you may doubt me for just a moment. At that moment, I felt a burning sensation in the middle of my back. A hot feeling that radiated outward. I looked around to find the source of it, and there was Celia across the room, staring a hole in the middle of my back. She wore a terrifying, angry glare. I looked at her, rolled my eyes resentfully, and turned away. I heard her book slam shut, and she stomped out of the room. I looked over at her as she passed and shook my head condescendingly.

How was that for handling a Crucial Conversation? I could not have done worse!

Can you see the irony in Joseph's story? When he came home after a long week of travel, guess what he wanted most? Time with the love of his life. And when he walked into the house, guess what Celia wanted most? Time with the love of her life. And yet both behaved in ways that got them the opposite. Why? Because both were hostage to their stories. In the moment, both believed their stories were accurate, and neither realized that their stories were creating their reality.

For example, when Joseph felt the burning sensation and observed Celia's expression, he told himself that Celia was unappreciative. She was judgmental. She was trying to control him. In his story, he justified answering the phone by thinking, "I've been working hard all week, and this is the treatment I get!" As a result, he felt defensive and resentful. That led to his ill-fated eye roll. The result? Celia closes her book loudly and leaves the room. In this moment, Joseph would argue his story is true: "Celia *is* judging me. And she *is* being unappreciative!" While there might be truth to Joseph's claim, what he's missing is the fact that he is part of the story. His actions helped Celia to tell the kind of story that created upset emotions that led to her behavior. He was a full partner in the downward spiral.

Be careful when you argue for your story that you first examine whether you might be creating the reality you claim to describe.

So why master your stories? Because it's a necessary step on the path toward what you really want.

SKILLS FOR MASTERING OUR STORIES

What's the most effective way to come up with different stories? The *best* at dialogue find a way to first slow down and then take charge of their Path to Action. Here's how:

Retrace Your Path

To slow down the lightning-quick storytelling process and the subsequent flow of adrenaline, retrace your Path to Action—one element at a time. This calls for a bit of mental gymnastics. First you have to stop what you're currently doing. Then you have to get in touch with why you're doing it. Here's how to retrace your path:

- **(Act)** Notice your behavior. Ask:

  "Am I acting out my concerns rather than talking them out?"

84

- **(Feel)** Put your feelings into words. Ask:

  "What emotions are encouraging me to act this way?"

- **(Tell story)** Analyze your stories. Ask:

  "What story is creating these emotions?"

- **(See/hear)** Get back to the facts. Ask:

  "What have I seen or heard that supports this story? What have I seen or heard that conflicts with this story?"

By retracing your path one element at a time, you put yourself in a position to think about, question, and change any or all of the elements.

Notice Your Behavior

Why would you stop and retrace your Path to Action in the first place? Certainly if you're constantly stopping what you're doing and looking for your underlying motive and thoughts, you won't even be able to put on your shoes without thinking about it for who knows how long. You'll die of analysis paralysis. Instead, consider two situations that can be cues to you that it is time to take a pause and retrace your Path to Action:

1. **Bad results.** You're not happy with the results you are getting. You're in a situation and don't like the outcome. You'd like to be promoted, but it's not happening. You'd like to enjoy time with your family, but every time you're at extended family gatherings, tempers flare. Whatever the situation, if you are not happy with the outcome, start by looking at how you behaved and the Path to Action that led to your behavior.

2. **Tough emotions.** You're feeling negative emotions. Strong ones. This is one of the best cues that it is time to retrace your path. If you're angry, frustrated, hurt, upset, or irritated, this is a great cue to ask why. Why am I feeling this way, and how is this feeling causing me to act?

But looking isn't enough. You must take an *honest* look at what you're doing. If you tell yourself a story that your aggressive behavior is a "necessary tactic," you won't see the need to reconsider your actions. If you immediately jump in with "They started it," or otherwise find yourself rationalizing your behavior, you also won't feel compelled to change. Rather than stop and review what you're doing, you'll tell self-justifying stories to yourself and others.

When an unhelpful story is driving your behavior, stop and consider how others would see your actions. For example, if the scene was livestreamed on social media, how would you look? How would a disinterested third party describe your behavior?

Not only do those who are best at Crucial Conversations notice when they're slipping out of dialogue, but they're also able to admit it. They *don't* wallow in self-doubt, but they *do* admit the problem and begin to take corrective action. The moment they realize they're killing dialogue, they review their own Path to Action.

Put Your Feelings into Words

As skilled individuals retrace their own Path to Action, they move from admitting their own unhealthy behavior to verbalizing their emotions. At first glance this task sounds easy. "I'm angry!" you think to yourself. What could be easier?

Actually, identifying your emotions is more difficult than you might imagine. In fact, many people are emotionally illiterate. When asked to describe how they're feeling, they use words such as "bad" or "angry" or "scared"—which would be OK if these were accurate descriptors, but often they're not. Individuals say they're angry when, in fact, they're feeling a mix of embarrassment and surprise. Or they suggest they're unhappy when they're feeling violated. Perhaps they suggest they're upset when they're really feeling humiliated and hurt.

Since life doesn't consist of a series of vocabulary tests, you might wonder what difference words can make. But words do matter.

Knowing what you're really feeling helps you take a more accurate look at what is going on and why. For instance, you're far more likely to take an honest look at the story you're telling yourself if you admit you're feeling both embarrassed and surprised rather than simply angry.

When you take the time to precisely articulate what you're feeling, you begin to put a little bit of daylight between you and the emotion. This distance lets you move from being hostage to the emotion to being an observer of it. When you can hold it at a little distance from yourself, you can examine it, study it, and begin to change it. But that process can't begin until you name it.

How about you? When experiencing strong emotions, do you stop and think about what you're feeling? If so, do you use a rich vocabulary, or do you mostly draw from terms such as "OK," "bummed out," "ticked off," or "frustrated"? Second, do you talk openly with others about how you feel? Do you willingly talk with loved ones about what's going on inside you? Third, in so doing, do you take the time to get below the easy-to-say emotions and accurately identify those that take more vulnerability to acknowledge (like shame, hurt, fear, and inadequacy)?

It's important to get in touch with your feelings, and to do so, you may want to expand your emotional vocabulary.

Analyze Your Stories

Question your feelings and stories. Once you've identified what you're feeling, stop and ask if, given the circumstances, it's the *right* feeling. Meaning, of course, are you telling the right story?

The first step to regaining emotional control is to challenge the illusion that what you're feeling is the only *right* emotion under the circumstances. This may be the hardest step, but it's also the most important one. By questioning our feelings, we open ourselves up to question our stories. We challenge the comfortable conclusion that our story is right and true. We willingly question whether our emotions (very real) and the story behind them (only one of many possible explanations) are accurate.

At this point, something overpowering inside us often protests: "Wait just a minute here. I shouldn't have to change my story. My story is accurate. It is true! I am right!"

This is the emotional equivalent of a Fool's Choice. It argues that stories are either right or wrong. That's rarely the case. More often than not, our stories are more or less accurate. For example, Maria might be right that Louis holds sexist biases about the influence of women. But that might not be *all* that's going on in this episode. What if Louis just got a bad performance review in which his boss admonished him to "have more of a voice." Would Maria feel differently if she knew this was *also* a part of what's happening? Furthermore, there are often subtleties embedded even in our "accurate" stories. For example, Maria's story could say that Louis's sexism is an unforgivable offense, or that it's a changeable human failing. That small distinction could lead her to either condemn him or attempt to influence him.

As we said before, any set of facts can be used to tell an *infinite* number of stories. The more we accept responsibility for the stories we tell, the more nuanced and effective our emotional responses become.

Get Back to the Facts

Sometimes you fail to question your stories because you see them as immutable facts. When you generate stories in the blink of an eye, you can get so caught up in the moment that you begin to believe your stories are facts. They *feel* like facts. You confuse subjective conclusions with steel-hard data points. For example, in trying to ferret out facts from story, Maria might say: "He's a misogynistic jerk!—that's a fact! Ask anyone who has seen how he treats me!"

"He's a misogynistic jerk" is not a fact. It's the story that Maria created to give meaning to the facts. The facts could mean just about anything. As we said earlier, others could watch Maria's interactions with Louis and walk away with different stories.

The best way to liberate yourself from an overpowering story is to separate facts from story. When trying to strip out story, it helps to test your ideas against a simple criterion: Can you *see* or *hear* this thing you're calling a fact? Was it an actual behavior?

For example, it is a fact that Louis "gave 95 percent of the presentation and answered all but one question." This is specific, objective, and verifiable. Any two people watching the meeting would make the same observation. However, the statement "He doesn't trust me" is a conclusion. It explains what you *think*, not what the other person *did*. Conclusions are subjective.

Spot the story by watching for "hot" words. To avoid confusing story with fact, watch for "hot" terms. For example, when assessing the facts, you might say, "She scowled at me" or "He made a sarcastic comment." Words such as "scowl" and "sarcastic" are hot terms. They express judgments and attributions that, in turn, create strong emotions. They are story, not fact. Notice how much different it is when you say, "Her eyes pinched shut and her lips tightened," as opposed to, "She scowled at me." In Maria's case, she suggested that Louis was controlling and didn't respect her. Had she focused on his behavior (he talked a lot and met with the boss one-on-one), this less volatile description would have allowed for any number of interpretations. For example, perhaps Louis was nervous, concerned, or unsure of himself.

Removing hot words and getting down to basic facts is harder than it sounds. For example, as Maria works to separate fact from story, she might go through a few iterations of removing judgments:

- **First attempt (all story).** Louis violated our plan, stole my slides, and forced me to the sidelines.
- **Second attempt (some facts).** Louis stole 10 of the slides I was supposed to cover and never once looked at me to answer questions.

- **Third attempt (more facts).** Louis covered 10 of the slides we previously agreed I would cover. When questions were asked, he answered all of them.

Scan for other facts. Once we start to tell a story ("Louis is a power-hungry weasel!"), we start to selectively see the evidence or facts that reinforce our story, and we overlook facts that contradict our story. We believe our story and want to continue to believe it. Thus, we only "see" that which helps us continue to believe. As we retrace our path and get back to the facts, we need to take another look at all the facts. Were there things that we, in the throes of our story, overlooked?

For example, if Maria has previously told herself a story about Louis, she'll unconsciously be looking for facts that back that story up. We all like to be right. So we look for confirming data, and we overlook or dismiss anything that contradicts it. As Maria scans for additional facts, perhaps she notices that Louis works really well with Sina, a colleague she respects. Or that Louis praised Maria's work in a team meeting last month.

As she liberates herself from the need to defend her story, Maria's list of facts might grow to include:

- **Fourth attempt (even more facts).** Louis covered 10 of the slides we previously agreed I would cover. And I let him. When questions were asked, he answered them without checking if I wanted to. And I did not step in to offer my view.

As you scan for other facts to complete the picture, be sure to ask, "What facts are there that contradict my story?"

Watch for Three "Clever" Stories

As you learn to question and analyze your stories, pay close attention to an insidious and common type of story: the self-justifying story. For example, you're faced with a Crucial Conversation. Rather than engaging in productive dialogue, you either shut down or push back. Recognizing on some level your own bad behavior, you quickly come up with a perfectly plausible reason why what you did was OK: "Of course I yelled at him. Did you see what he did? He deserved it." Or "Hey, don't you dare judge me for not speaking up. I don't have a choice. I have to keep this job."

We call these imaginative and self-serving concoctions "clever stories." They're clever because they allow us to feel good about behaving badly. Better yet, they allow us to feel good about behaving badly even while achieving abysmal results.

When we feel a need to justify our ineffective behavior or disconnect ourselves from our bad results, we tend to tell our stories in three very predictable ways. Learn what the three are and how to counteract them, and you can take control of your emotional life.

Victim Stories—"It's Not My Fault"

The first of the clever stories is a Victim Story. Victim Stories, as you might imagine, make us out to be innocent sufferers. The theme is always the same. We are good, right, brilliant, or righteous, and other people or the world at large is aligned against us. We suffer through absolutely no fault of our own. We are innocent.

There is such a thing as an innocent victim. You're stopped in the street and held up at gunpoint. When an event such as this occurs, it's a sad fact, not a story. You *are* a victim.

But not all tales of victimization are so clear-cut and one-sided. Within most Crucial Conversations, when you tell a Victim Story, you intentionally ignore the role you have played in the problem. You tell your story in a way that judiciously avoids whatever *you* have done (or neglected to do) that might have contributed to the problem.

For instance, last week your boss took you off a big project, and it hurt your feelings. You complained to everyone about how bad you felt. What you did not explain was that you failed to let your boss know that you were behind on an important project, leaving him high and dry—which is why he removed you in the first place. This part of the story you leave out because, hey, he made you feel bad.

To help support your Victim Stories, you speak of nothing but your noble motives: "I took longer because I was trying to beat the standard specs." Then you tell yourself that you're being punished for your virtues, not your vices: "He just doesn't appreciate a person with my superb attention to detail." (This added twist turns you from victim into martyr. What a bonus!)

Villain Stories—"It's All Your Fault"

We create these nasty little tales by turning normal, decent human beings into villains. We impute bad motive, and then we tell everyone about the evils of the other party as if somehow we're doing the world a huge favor. We ignore any of our villains' virtues and turn their flaws into exaggerated indictments.

For example, we describe a boss who is zealous about quality as a "control freak." When our spouse is upset that *we* didn't keep a commitment, we see him or her as "inflexible and stubborn."

In Victim Stories we exaggerate our own innocence. In Villain Stories we overemphasize the other person's guilt or stupidity. We automatically assume the worst possible motives or grossest incompetence while ignoring any possible good or neutral intentions or skills a person may have. Often we'll dehumanize our villain further by replacing his or her name with a label. For example, "I can't believe that *bonehead* gave me bad materials again." By employing the handy label, we are now dealing not with a complex human being, but with a bonehead.

Not only do Villain Stories help us blame others for bad results; they also set us up to then do whatever we want to the "villains." After all, we can feel OK insulting or abusing a *bonehead* or a *lawyer*—whereas we might have to be more careful with a living, breathing person. Then when we fail to get the results we really want, we stay stuck in our ineffective behavior because, after all, look who we're dealing with!

Sometimes we go beyond villainizing individuals to villainizing entire communities of people: "Those yahoos in engineering have no idea what it takes to sell our product." "Lawyers! You can't trust a single one." Taking an individual human being, lumping the person into a broad category, and then rejecting that entire group of people allows us to both be angry at them and dismiss them, all at once. Heartbreakingly, villainizing groups and communities continually perpetuates mistreatment and oppression.

Watch for the double standard. When you pay attention to Victim and Villain Stories and catch them for what they are—unfair caricatures—you begin to see the terrible double standard we use when our emotions are out of control. When *we* make mistakes, we tell a Victim Story by claiming our intentions were innocent and pure: "Sure I was late getting home and didn't call you, but I couldn't let the team down!" On the other hand, when *others* do things that hurt or inconvenience us, we tell Villain Stories in which we *invent* terrible motives or exaggerate flaws for others based on how their actions affected us: "You are so thoughtless! You could have called me and told me you were going to be late."

Helpless Stories—"There's Nothing Else I Can Do"

Finally come Helpless Stories. In these fabrications we make ourselves out to be powerless to do anything healthy or helpful. We convince ourselves that there are no healthy alternatives for dealing with our predicament, which justifies the action we're about to take. A Helpless Story might suggest, "If I didn't yell at my son, he wouldn't listen." Or on the flip side, "If I told the boss this, he would just be defensive—so of course I say nothing!" While Villain and Victim Stories look back to explain why we're in the situation we're in, Helpless Stories look forward to explain why we can't do anything to change our situation.

It's particularly easy to act helpless when we turn others' behavior into fixed and unchangeable traits. For example, when we decide our colleague is a "control freak" (Villain Story), we are less inclined to give her feedback because, after all, control freaks like her don't accept feedback (Helpless Story). Nothing we can do will change that fact.

As you can see, Helpless Stories often stem from Villain Stories and typically offer us nothing more than Fool's Choices—we can either be honest and ruin the relationship or stay silent and suffer.

Why We Tell Clever Stories

By now it should be clear that clever stories cause us problems. A reasonable question at this point is, "If they're so terribly hurtful, why do we *ever* tell clever stories?" There are two reasons:

Clever stories match reality. Sometimes the stories we tell are accurate. The other person is trying to cause us harm, we are innocent victims, or maybe we really can't do much about the problem. It can happen. It's not common, but it can happen.

Clever stories justify our actions. More often than not, our conclusions transform from reasonable explanations to clever stories when they conveniently excuse us from any responsibility—when, in reality, we have been partially responsible. The other person isn't bad and wrong, and we aren't right and good. The truth lies somewhere in the middle. However, if we can make others out as wrong and ourselves out as right, we're off the hook. Better yet, once we've demonized others, we can even insult and abuse them if we want.

Our need to tell clever stories often starts with our own sellouts. Like it or not, we usually don't begin telling stories that justify our actions until we have done something that we feel a need to justify.

We sell out when we consciously act against our own sense of what's right. And if we don't admit to our errors, we inevitably look for ways to justify them. That's when we begin to tell clever stories. Recall that when Joseph walked in the door after a week of travel and heard the phone ring, he knew what he should do. He had a clear call of conscience to ignore the phone and focus on his wife. But he didn't. *That* was the moment he began formulating a clever story. He turned Celia into a villain ("She is so unappreciative!") and himself into a victim ("I've been working hard all week and deserve understanding!") and voilà! He felt justified in behaving terribly and blamed Celia for ruining their reunion.

Let's look at another example of a sellout: You're driving in heavy traffic. You begin to pass cars that are attempting to merge into your lane. A car very near you has accelerated and is entering your lane. A thought strikes you that you *should* let him in. It's the nice thing to do, and you'd want someone to let you in. But you don't. You accelerate forward and close the gap. What happens next? You begin to have thoughts like these: "He can't just crowd in on me. What a jerk! I've been fighting this traffic a long time. Besides, I've got an important appointment to get to." And so on.

This story makes you the innocent victim and the other person the nasty villain. Under the influence of this story, you now feel justified in not doing what you originally thought you should have done. You also ignore what you would think of others who did the same thing to you—"That jerk didn't let me in!"

Consider an example more related to Crucial Conversations. There is a new member of your team at work. He is significantly less experienced than you and eager to learn. He keeps coming to you and asking questions. Sometimes he asks the same question he asked yesterday. You are starting to get tired of holding his hand. And he is taking so much time that your own work is backing up. You know you should start saying no to many of his requests and direct him to other resources, but you don't. Instead, you start giving him really curt or abrupt answers, hoping he will get the hint. He doesn't. Your annoyance turns to resentment. You stop responding to his emails and set your instant message tool to "Away," hoping to avoid him entirely. When he notices your behavior and asks you why, you dodge with a half-truth: "I'm just really busy." You feel a little guilty about avoiding him. In an effort to feel better about your actions, you start complaining to other team members about all the time he is taking from you and how much help he needs. Who hired this guy anyway?

Notice the order of the events in both of these examples. What came first, the story or the sellout? Did you convince yourself of the other driver's selfishness and *then* not let him in? Of course not. You had no reason to think he was selfish until you needed an excuse for your own selfish behavior. You didn't start telling clever stories until *after* you failed to do something you knew you should have done. Your coworker's needs didn't become a source of resentment until you became part of the problem. You got upset because you sold out. And the clever story helped you feel good about being rude.

Sellouts are often not big events. In fact, they can be so small that they're easy for us to overlook when we're crafting our clever stories. Here are some common ones:

- You believe you should help someone, but don't.
- You believe you should apologize, but don't.
- You believe you should stay late to finish up on a commitment, but go home instead.
- You say yes when you know you should say no, then hope no one follows up to see if you keep your commitment.
- You believe you should talk to someone about concerns you have with him or her, but don't.
- You do less than your share and think you should acknowledge it, but say nothing, knowing no one else will bring it up either.

- You believe you should listen respectfully to feedback, but become defensive instead.
- You see problems with a plan someone presents and think you should speak up, but don't.
- You fail to complete an assignment on time and believe you should let others know, but don't.
- You know you have information a coworker could use, but keep it to yourself.

Even small sellouts like these get us started telling clever stories. When we don't admit to our own mistakes, we obsess about others' faults, our innocence, and our powerlessness to do anything other than what we're already doing. We tell a clever story when we want self-justification more than results. Of course, self-justification is not what we *really* want, but we certainly act as if it is.

With that sad fact in mind, let's focus on what we really want. Let's look at the final Master My Stories skill.

Tell the Rest of the Story

Once we've learned to recognize the clever stories we tell ourselves, we can move to the final Master My Stories skill. The *best* at dialogue recognize that they're telling clever stories, stop, and then do what it takes to tell a *useful* story. A useful story, by definition, creates emotions that lead to healthy action—such as dialogue.

And what transforms a clever story into a useful one? The rest of the story. That's because clever stories have one characteristic in common: They're incomplete. Clever stories omit crucial information about us, about others, and about our options. Only by including all these essential details can clever stories be transformed into useful ones.

What's the best way to fill in the missing details? Quite simply, it's done by turning victims into actors, villains into humans, and the helpless into the able. Here's how:

Turn victims into actors. If you notice that you're talking about yourself as an innocent victim (and you weren't held up at gunpoint), ask:

> *"What am I pretending not to notice about my role in the problem?"*

This question jars you into facing up to the fact that maybe, just maybe, you did something to help cause the problem. Instead of being a victim, you were an actor. This doesn't necessarily mean you had malicious motives. Perhaps your contribution was merely a thoughtless omission. Nonetheless, you contributed.

For example, a coworker constantly leaves the harder or noxious tasks for you to complete. You've frequently complained to friends and loved ones about being exploited. The parts you leave out of the story are that you smile broadly when your boss compliments you for your willingness to take on challenging jobs, and you've never said anything to your coworker. You've hinted, but that's about it.

More often than not, when faced with persistent or recurrent problems, the role we are playing (and are pretending not to notice) is one of silent complicity. The problem has been going on for a while and we have said . . . nothing. Our role is silence.

The first step in telling the rest of this story would be to add these important facts to your account. By asking what role you've played, you begin to realize how selective your perception has been. You become aware of how you've minimized your own mistakes while you've exaggerated the role of others.

Turn villains into humans. When you find yourself labeling or otherwise vilifying others, stop and ask:

> *"Why would a reasonable, rational, and decent person do what this person is doing?"*

This particular question humanizes others. As we search for plausible answers to it, our emotions soften. Empathy often replaces judgment, and depending upon how *we've* treated *others*, personal accountability replaces self-justification.

For instance, that coworker who seems to conveniently miss out on the tough jobs told you recently that she could see you were struggling with an important assignment, and yesterday (while you were tied up on a pressing task) she pitched in and completed the job for you. You were instantly suspicious. She was trying to make you look bad by completing a high-profile job. How dare she pretend to be helpful when her real goal was to discredit you while tooting her own horn! Well, that's the story you've told yourself.

But what if she really were a reasonable, rational, and decent person? What if she had no motive other than to give you a hand? Isn't it a bit early to be vilifying her? And if you do, don't you run the risk of ruining a relationship? Might you go off half-cocked, accuse her, and then learn you were wrong?

Our purpose for asking why a reasonable, rational, and decent person might be acting a certain way is *not* to excuse others for any bad things they may be doing. If they are, indeed, guilty, we'll have time to deal with that later. The purpose of the humanizing question is to deal with our own stories and emotions. It provides us with still another tool for working on ourselves, first by providing a variety of possible reasons for the other person's behavior.

In fact, with experience and maturity, we learn to worry less about others' intent and more about the *effect* others' actions are having on us. No longer are we in the game of rooting out unhealthy motives. When we reflect on alternative motives, not only do we soften our emotions, but equally important, we relax our absolute certainty long enough to allow for dialogue—the only reliable way of discovering others' genuine motives.

Turn the helpless into the able. Finally, when you catch yourself bemoaning your own helplessness, you can tell the complete story by returning to your original motive. To do so, stop and ask:

"What do I really want? For me? For others? For the relationship?"

Then break free of the Fool's Choice that's made you feel helpless to choose anything other than going on the attack or staying silent. Do this by asking:

"What should I do right now to move toward what I really want?"

For example, you now find yourself insulting your coworker for not pitching in with a tough job. Your coworker seems surprised at your strong and "out of the blue" reaction. In fact, she's staring at you as if you've slipped a cog. You, of course, have told yourself that she is purposely avoiding noxious tasks and that, despite your helpful hints, she has made no changes.

"I have to get brutal," you tell yourself. "I don't like it, but if I don't offend her, I'll be stuck." You've strayed from what you really want—to share work equally *and* to have a good relationship. You've given up on half your goals by making a Fool's Choice: "Oh well, better to offend her than to be made a fool."

What should you be doing instead? Openly, honestly, and effectively discussing the problem—not taking potshots and then justifying yourself. When you refuse to make yourself helpless, you're forced to hold yourself accountable for using your dialogue skills rather than bemoaning your weakness.

THE HOSTAGE NEGOTIATOR

When we humanize others, we're not excusing bad behavior or motives. We're helping ourselves be in a place to have a meaningful and successful Crucial Conversation. Coauthor Ron McMillan learned about the value of this principle from a man in a very high-risk occupation. Hear about it in the video *The Hostage Negotiator* at crucialconversations.com.

MARIA'S NEW STORY

To see how this all fits together, let's circle back to Maria. Let's assume she's retraced her Path to Action and separated the facts from the stories. Doing this has helped her realize that the story she told was incomplete, defensive, and hurtful. When she watched for the three clever stories, she saw them with painful clarity. Now she's ready to tell the rest of the story. So she asks herself:

- "What am I pretending not to notice about my role in the problem?"

  "When I found out that Louis was holding project meetings without me, I felt like I should ask him about why I wasn't included. I believed that if I did, I could open a dialogue that would help us work better together. But then I didn't, and as my resentment grew, I was even less interested in broaching the subject. During the presentation, I chose not to interrupt when he started covering my slides. And I sulked rather than speaking up when he failed to invite me to take questions."

- "Why would a reasonable, rational, and decent person do what Louis is doing?"

  "He really cares about producing good-quality work. Maybe he doesn't realize that I'm as committed to the success of the project as he is. His actions in the meeting might have been about his nervousness rather than judgment of me."

- "What do I really want?"

  "I want a respectful relationship with Louis. And I want to be treated with respect."

- "What should I do right now to move toward what I really want?"

  "I'd make an appointment to sit down with Louis and talk about how the presentation went and how we work together."

As we tell the rest of the story, we free ourselves from the poisoning effects of unhealthy emotions. Best of all, as we regain control and move back to dialogue, we become masters of our own emotions rather than hostages.

And what about Maria? What did she actually do? She scheduled a meeting with Louis. After Maria explained her expectations of and views about the project, Louis apologized for not including her in meetings with the boss. He explained that he was trying to give the boss a heads-up on some controversial parts of the presentation—and realized in retrospect that he shouldn't have done this without her. He also apologized for dominating during the presentation. Maria learned from the conversation that Louis tends to talk more when he gets nervous. He suggested that they each be responsible for either the first or second half of the presentation and stick to their assignments so he would be less likely to crowd her out. The discussion ended with both of them understanding the other's perspective and Louis promising to be more sensitive in the future.

My Crucial Conversation: Marion B.

After 25 years in my organization, I was one move away from a cabinet-level position. However, no matter how many times I applied and interviewed for such positions, I was never selected. As I was passed over again and again, I began to tell myself stories about it. But I said nothing.

After becoming a trainer for Crucial Conversations, I took another look at my situation, and I realized there was a conversation I was not having. I had not asked the leaders in my organization what was preventing me from moving forward.

It was tough medicine, but as I learned about mastering my story, I realized that at first I had remained silent by telling myself it was just bad luck. As the luck story wore thin, it became a "politics" story—others were better at buttering up the right people. I had lost out because I had "integrity." My Victim and Villain Stories were keeping me silent and resentful. After many hours of reflection I got to a new story: "Part of being passed over was because I had not asked for feedback." I was no longer a victim; I was an actor. And I decided to take action.

The conversation was tough. I was told that in order to move to a cabinet-level position, I would have to first take a cabinet-level position in a smaller organization. That information rang true. But I didn't like it. However, I was now in a position to make a decision. So I did. I left my organization and got a job leading a department four times larger than the one where I previously worked.

Had I not finally faced my story, I would not have gotten the results I wanted most.

SUMMARY: MASTER MY STORIES

If strong emotions are keeping you stuck in silence or violence, try these steps:

Retrace Your Path

- **Examine your behavior.** If you find yourself moving away from dialogue, ask yourself what you're really doing.
- **Put your feelings into words.** Learn to accurately identify and name the emotions behind your story. Ask:

  "What emotions are encouraging me to act this way?"

- **Spot your story.** Identify your story. Ask:

  "What story must I be telling to create these emotions? What story is creating these emotions?"

- **Separate fact from story.** Abandon your absolute certainty by distinguishing between hard facts and your invented story. Ask:

  "What evidence do I have to support this story?"

- **Watch for clever stories.** Victim, Villain, and Helpless Stories sit at the top of the list.

Tell the Rest of the Story

- Ask:

  "What am I pretending not to notice about my role in the problem?"

  "Why would a reasonable, rational, and decent person do this?"

  "What do I really want?"

  "What should I do right now to move toward what I really want?"

PART II

HOW TO OPEN YOUR MOUTH

At this point you are mentally and emotionally prepared for a healthy conversation. Now it's time to open your mouth and speak. But how? What do you say first? Second? Third? And how can you be prepared for the inevitable land mines you'll run across once you do?

The skills in this section will help you be prepared for surprises (Chapter 6, "Learn to Look"), reduce the chance others will become defensive (Chapter 7, "Make It Safe"), make your points in a way that invites interest rather than defensiveness (Chapter 8, "STATE My Path"), and discover the meaning others have to offer (Chapter 9, "Explore Others' Paths") without it getting under your skin (Chapter 10, "Retake Your Pen").

6

LEARN TO LOOK

How to Notice When Safety Is at Risk

Let's start this chapter by visiting a failed Crucial Conversation. You and your team have been working hard on a proposal for a company acquisition. Your manager is now taking the proposal to the steering committee. He has invited you to "sit in on" the meeting. He has made it clear that your role here is to listen and observe. You're excited for a couple of reasons. First, you believe in your team's recommendation and want to see how the steering committee responds. Second, this is the first time you'll see the organization's leadership team in action. It's exhilarating to be included.

The first thing you notice as you take your chair next to a wall on one side of the room is where all the executives are sitting. Not surprisingly, the CEO, Corinne, is at the head of the rather large table. There doesn't necessarily seem to be much order to where everyone else sits, but you do notice that Marco, the CFO, is at the far end of the table. You have heard through the grapevine that those two have a bit of a contentious relationship.

The meeting opens, and Corinne asks your manager to present the proposal. He does a great job outlining the recommendations as his colleagues listen attentively. He opens it up for questions. Someone, you aren't sure who, asks a probing but friendly question. Your manager responds, but before he can ask for other questions, Corinne jumps in with her opinion. The discussion continues like this for some time: Someone makes a comment; Corinne responds. Another comment; another interjection from Corinne. You notice that Corinne comments after virtually every other person's comments, never letting the discussion go too far without her input.

Finally, Marco speaks up. He summarizes what he has heard, clarifies that he understands Corinne's position, and then forcefully tells her why she is wrong. She pushes back on him. He pushes back on her. Everyone is watching the tense exchange between the two. Just when you think they're about to start yelling, Corinne pulls back, tables the discussion, and ends the meeting. Marco pushes his chair back from the table with the force and urgency of someone jumping out of the way of an oncoming bus and stalks from the room without saying anything to anyone.

As you and your manager take the elevator back down to your floor, you say, "Wow! Is it often like that?"

"Pretty much," he responds. "It always seems to start off well enough, but then inevitably it deteriorates. Those two just can't work together. From the moment Marco opens his mouth, it's a train wreck."

"How so?" you ask, wondering what your manager is seeing.

"Well, by the end it was easy to see how upset they each were. They were constantly interrupting and talking over each other, their voices getting louder and louder. But even before that, from Marco's first comment, I knew it would go badly. He starts with such absolutes: 'It's always been like this . . . That will never work . . .' The guy is probably the smartest person on the team, and he knows it. That language? 'Always,' 'never,' etc.? It inevitably gets Corinne's back up."

You think about this for a minute and then say: "I definitely agree. The warning signs were there from the moment Marco started talking. But you know . . . I think there were a few things that happened even earlier that set the conversation off in the wrong direction."

"Really?" your manager replies with surprise. "I thought it was going pretty well until Marco started talking. What did you see before that?"

"Well," you start thoughtfully, "it struck me as interesting that Corinne commented on almost everyone else's comments. You would say something; then she would say something. Then someone else; then Corinne again. Sometimes, she even jumped in and cut someone off in order to get her comment in."

"Oh sure," your manager says. "But that is just how Corinne is. She's really passionate about things and wants to engage in dialogue with all of us."

"Hmmm . . . ," you say. "Well, that may be true . . . that she says she wants to have everyone weigh in. But I think her jumping in all the time is impacting the conversation. She is really controlling the pace and direction of the dialogue. I wonder if that's part of what makes Marco come in so strong."

"I've never thought about it. Or really even noticed that before," your manager says. "I guess I'll have to watch for it next time."

The elevator dings, and you head in separate directions.

WATCH FOR CONDITIONS

The sooner you notice you're not in dialogue, the easier it is to get back and the lower the costs. The sad corollary is that the longer it takes to notice you're not in dialogue, the harder it is to get back and the higher the costs.

Yet most of us have trouble noticing the early warning signs of declining communication. During Crucial Conversations, the key to maintaining dialogue is to learn to dual-process. Not only do you have to be attentive to the content of the conversation (what is being said), but you also have to skillfully observe the process (how it's being said). When stakes get high, we get so caught up in what we're saying that it can be nearly impossible to pull ourselves out of the argument. As a result, we don't see what's happening to ourselves and to others. Even when we are startled by what's going on, enough so that we think: "Yipes! This has turned ugly. Now what?," we may not know what to look for in order to turn things around. We may not see enough of what's happening.

How could we be smack-dab in the middle of a heated debate and not really see what's going on? A metaphor might help. It's like fly-fishing for the first time with an experienced angler. Your guide keeps telling you to cast your fly six feet upstream from that brown trout "just out there." Only you can't see a brown trout "just out there." She can. That's because she knows what to look for. You *think* you do. You think you need to look for a brown trout. In reality, you need to look for the distorted image of a brown trout that's underwater while the sun is reflecting in your eyes. You have to look for elements other than the thing that your parents have stuffed and mounted over the fireplace. It takes both knowledge and practice to know what to look for and then actually see it.

So what do you look for when caught in the middle of a Crucial Conversation? What do you need to see in order to catch problems before they become too severe? It helps to watch for three different conditions: the moment a conversation turns crucial, signs that people don't feel safe (silence or violence), and your own Style Under Stress. Let's consider each of these conversation killers in turn.

Learn to Spot Crucial Conversations

First, stay alert for the moment a conversation turns from a routine or harmless discussion into a crucial one. In a similar vein, as you anticipate entering a tough conversation, be aware of the fact that you're about to enter the danger zone. Otherwise you can easily get sucked into silly games before you realize what's happened. And as we suggested earlier, the further you stray off track, the harder it can be to return and the higher the costs.

To help catch problems early, reprogram your mind to pay attention to the signs that suggest you're in a Crucial Conversation. Some people first notice *physical* signals. Think about what happens to your body when conversations get tough. Everyone is a little bit different. What are your cues? Maybe your stomach gets tight or your eyes get dry. Whatever they are, learn to look at them as signs to step back, slow down, and Start with Heart before things get out of hand.

Others notice their *emotions* before they notice signs in their body. They realize they are scared, hurt, defensive, or angry and are beginning to react to or suppress these feelings. These emotions can also be great cues to tell you to step back, slow down, and take steps to turn your brain back on.

Some people's first cue is *behavioral*. For them it's like an out-of-body experience. They see themselves raising their voice, pointing their finger like a loaded weapon, or becoming very quiet. It's only then that they realize how they're feeling.

So take a moment to think about some of your toughest conversations. What cues can you use to recognize that your brain is beginning to disengage and you're at risk of moving away from healthy dialogue?

Learn to Look for Safety Problems

People who are gifted at dialogue keep a constant vigil on *safety*. They pay attention to the content, and they watch for signs that people are becoming fearful. When friends, loved ones, or colleagues move away from healthy dialogue—by either forcing their opinions into the pool or purposely keeping their ideas out of the pool—the *best* at dialogue immediately turn their attention to why others might not feel safe.

When it's safe, you can say anything. Here's why gifted communicators keep a close eye on safety. Dialogue calls for the free flow of meaning—period. And nothing kills the flow of meaning like fear. When you fear people aren't buying into your ideas, you start pushing too hard. When you fear you may be harmed in some way, you start withdrawing and hiding. Both these reactions—fight and flight—are motivated by the same emotion: fear. On the other hand, if you make it safe enough, you can talk about almost anything, and people will listen. If you don't fear that you're being attacked or humiliated, you yourself can hear almost anything and not become defensive.

This is a pretty remarkable claim. Think about it. We're suggesting that people rarely become defensive simply because of *what* you're saying. They only become defensive when they no longer feel safe, or when they question *why* you're saying the things you are. Specifically, they begin to speculate about either your respect ("Is this message a sign of disrespect?"), your intent ("Does this message tell me you have malicious motives toward me?"), or both. Either way, the problem is not the *content* of your message, but the *condition* of the conversation. As we saw earlier, from the time we are quite small we begin to conclude that you can't be both honest and respectful simultaneously. In essence, we conclude that there are some messages you just can't give to some people. And over time, that list of messages gets longer and longer until we find ourselves handling most Crucial Conversations badly. If what we're suggesting here is true, then the problem is not the message. The problem is that you and I fail to help others feel safe hearing the message. If you can learn to see when people start to feel unsafe, you can take action to fix it. That means the first challenge is to simply *see* and *understand* that safety is at risk.

Think about your own experience. Can you remember receiving really tough feedback from someone at some point in your life and not becoming defensive? Instead, you absorbed the feedback. You reflected on it. You allowed it to influence you. If so, ask yourself why. Why in this instance were you able to take potentially threatening feedback so well? If you're like the rest of us, it's because you believed the other person had your best interest in mind. In addition, you respected the other person's opinion. You felt *safe* receiving the feedback because you trusted the motives and ability of the other person. You didn't need to defend yourself from what was being said—even if you didn't like what the person was saying!

On the other hand, if you don't feel safe, you can't take any feedback. It's as if the pool of meaning has a lid on it: "What do you mean I look good? Is that some kind of joke? Are you insulting me?" When you don't feel safe, even well-intended comments are suspect.

Safety isn't synonymous with comfort. At this point, it is worth noting that feeling safe in a conversation is not synonymous with feeling comfortable. We'll define safety more in the next chapter. But for now we want to be clear about what safety *isn't*. Crucial Conversations are, by definition, hard conversations. We and others have to stretch in these conversations, often venturing into new territory and feeling some degree of vulnerability. The measure of whether a conversation is safe is not how comfortable I feel. It is whether meaning is flowing. Do I, and others, feel like we can share our meaning, have that meaning heard, and also listen honestly and respectfully to each other? If you can do that, if meaning is flowing honestly and respectfully, you know safety is there.

When it's unsafe, you start to go blind. As we know, when your emotions start cranking up, key brain functions start shutting down. When you feel genuinely threatened, your peripheral vision actually narrows until you can scarcely see beyond what's right in front of you.

By pulling yourself out of the content of an argument and looking for signs that safety is at risk, you reengage your brain, and your full vision returns. As we suggested earlier, when you give yourself a new problem to consider (keep alert for signs that safety is at risk!), you affect your brain functioning. Your higher reasoning centers stay more active, and you're far less likely to be dumbed down and far more likely to succeed in your Crucial Conversations.

Don't let safety problems lead you astray. When others begin to feel unsafe, they start acting in annoying ways. They may make fun of you, insult you, or steamroll you with their arguments. In such moments, you *should* be thinking to yourself: "Hey, they're feeling unsafe. I need to do something—maybe make it safer." Unfortunately, more often than not, instead of taking their attack as a sign that safety is at risk, you take it at its face—as an attack. "I'm under attack!" you think. Then the dumb part of your brain kicks in and you respond in kind. Or maybe you try to escape. Either way, you're not dual-processing and trying to restore safety. Instead, you're becoming part of the problem as you get pulled into the fight.

Imagine the magnitude of what we're suggesting here. We're asking you to fight your natural tendency to respond in kind, and instead think, "Ah, that's a sign that the other person feels unsafe." And then what? Do something to make it safe.

Just to be crystal clear, we are not asking you to tolerate abusive behavior. We are asking you to consider the cause of that behavior. Sure, some "jerks" are in fact truly jerks, deep down and all the way through. But let's be honest. Have you ever lost your temper? Yelled at someone in the heat of the moment? Interrupted someone when you just couldn't take it anymore? Used your power (as a parent, boss, or expert) inappropriately to get what you want? You know . . . acted like a jerk? Probably. We all have at times. And guess what? We aren't jerks. We're just people who, in a tough moment, responded to a lack of safety with aggression. We see it in ourselves. We need to give people the respect and grace to see it in them. Obviously this can be difficult. But it's worth it.

These skills are the pivot point for everything that follows in the process of creating dialogue. They're the gateway to gaining all the benefits that come to those who are skilled at Crucial Conversations. Imagine increased influence, enhanced relationships, stronger teams, and more effective leadership. Turn on your capacity to recognize and respond to safety problems.

In the next chapter, we'll explore how to respond. For now, simply learn to look for safety, and then be curious instead of angry or frightened. Learn to identify the two kinds of behavior that will clue you in to the fact that someone's feeling unsafe. We refer to them as silence and violence.

Silence and Violence

As people begin to feel unsafe, they start down one of two unhealthy paths. They move either to silence (withholding meaning from the pool) or to verbal violence (trying to force meaning in the pool). That part we know. But let's add a little more detail. Just as a little knowledge of what to look for can turn blurry water into a brown trout, knowing a few of the common forms of silence and violence helps you see safety problems when they first start to happen. That way you can step out, restore safety, and return to dialogue—before the damage is too great.

Silence. Silence consists of any act to purposely withhold information from the pool of meaning. It's almost always done as a means of avoiding potential problems, and it always restricts the flow of meaning. Methods range from playing verbal games to avoiding a person entirely. The three most common forms of silence are masking, avoiding, and withdrawing.

Masking consists of understating or selectively showing our true opinions. Sarcasm, sugarcoating, and couching are some of the more popular forms:

"I think your idea is, uh, brilliant. Yeah, that's it. I just worry that others won't catch the subtle nuances. Some ideas come before their time, so expect some, uh, minor resistance."

Meaning: *Your idea is insane, and people will fight it with their last breath.*

"Oh yeah, that'll work like a charm" (accompanied by an eye roll). "Offer people a discount, and they'll drive all the way across town just to save six cents on a box of soap."

Meaning: *What a dumb idea.*

Avoiding involves steering completely away from sensitive subjects. We talk, but without addressing the real issues:

"How does your new suit look? Well, you know that blue's my favorite color."

Meaning: *What happened? Did you buy your clothes at the circus?*

"Speaking of ideas for cost cutting, what if we diluted the coffee? Or used both sides of our copier paper?"

Meaning: *If I offer trivial suggestions, perhaps we can avoid discussing sensitive things like staff inefficiency.*

Withdrawing means pulling out of a conversation altogether. We either exit the conversation or exit the room:

"Excuse me. I've got to take this call."

Meaning: *I'd rather gnaw off my own arm than spend one more minute in this useless meeting.*

"Sorry, I'm not going to talk about how to split up the phone bill again. I'm not sure our friendship can stand another battle." (Exits.)

Meaning: *We can't talk about even the simplest of topics without arguing.*

Violence. Violence consists of any verbal strategy that attempts to convince or control others or compel them to your point of view. It violates safety by trying to force meaning into the pool. Methods range from name-calling and monologuing to making threats. The three most common forms are controlling, labeling, and attacking.

Controlling consists of coercing others to your way of thinking. It's done through either forcing your views on others or dominating the conversation by interrupting, overstating your facts, speaking in absolutes, changing subjects, or using directive questions, among other strategies:

> *"There's not a person in the world who hasn't bought one of these things. They're the perfect gift."*
>
> **Meaning:** *I can't justify spending our hard-earned savings on this expensive toy, but I really want it.*

> *"We tried their product, but it was an absolute disaster. Everyone knows that they can't deliver on time and that they offer the worst customer service on the planet."*
>
> **Meaning:** *I'm not certain of the real facts, so I'll use hyperbole to get your attention.*

Labeling is putting a label on people or ideas so we can dismiss them under a general stereotype or category:

"That idea? It might have worked in the 1990s. But no one who actually cares about quality and customer service would ever implement that kind of a plan today."

Meaning: *I can't argue my case on its merits, so to get what I want, I'll attack you personally.*

"Are you serious? Only a [insert name of the opposing political party] would think that's a good idea."

Meaning: *If I pretend that all people from the political persuasion opposing mine are somehow bad and wrong, I won't have to explain anything.*

Attacking speaks for itself. Your motive goes from winning the argument to making the other person suffer. Tactics include belittling and threatening:

"Try that stupid little stunt and see what happens."

Meaning: *I will get my way on this even if I have to bad-mouth you and threaten some vague punishment.*

"Don't listen to a word Jim is saying. I'm sorry, Jim, but I'm on to you. You're just trying to make it better for your team while making the rest of us suffer. I've seen you do it before. You're a real jerk, you know that? I'm sorry, but someone has to have the guts to tell it like it is."

Meaning: *To get my way, I'll say bad things about you and then pretend that I'm the only one with any integrity.*

Look for Your Style Under Stress

You've been paying attention to determine when a conversation turns crucial and to identify signs that safety is at risk. There is one more thing you need to watch: your own behavior. This is perhaps the most difficult element to watch closely. Most people have trouble pulling themselves away from the tractor beam of the argument at hand. After all, it's not like you can actually step out of your body and observe yourself. You're on the wrong side of your eyeballs.

Low self-monitors. The truth is, we all have trouble monitoring our own behavior at times. We usually lose any semblance of social sensitivity when we become so consumed with ideas and causes that we lose track of what we're doing. We try to bully our way through. We speak when we shouldn't. We withdraw into a punishing silence. We're basically the guy in the Jack Handey story quoted below:

> *People were always talking about how mean this guy was who lived on our block. But I decided to go see for myself. I went to his door, but he said he wasn't the mean guy, the mean guy lived in that house over there. "No, you stupid idiot," I said, "that's my house."*

Unfortunately, when you fail to monitor your own behavior, you can look pretty silly. For example, you're talking to your spouse about the fact that he or she left you sitting at the auto repair shop for over an hour. Your spouse says it was a simple misunderstanding and exclaims, "You don't have to get angry."

Then you utter those famous words: "I'm not angry!"

Of course, you're spraying spit as you shout out your denial, and the vein on your forehead has swelled to the size of a teenage python. You, quite naturally, don't see the inconsistency in your response. You're in the middle of the whole thing, and you don't appreciate it one bit when your spouse laughs at you.

Your Style Under Stress Test

What kind of a self-monitor are you? One good way to increase your self-awareness is to explore your Style Under Stress. What do you do when talking turns tough? To find out, fill out the survey on the following pages. Or for easier scoring, visit www.crucialconversations.com. It'll help you see what tactics you typically revert to in the midst of a Crucial Conversation. It'll also help you determine which parts of this book can be most helpful to you.

Instructions. The following questions explore how you *typically* respond when you're in the middle of a Crucial Conversation. Before answering, pick a specific relationship at work or at home. Then circle either T (True) or F (False) based on how you typically approach risky conversations in that relationship.

T F **1.** Rather than tell people exactly what I think, sometimes I rely on jokes, sarcasm, or snide remarks to let them know I'm frustrated.

T F **2.** When I've got something tough to bring up, I understate it rather than share my full opinion.

T F **3.** Sometimes when people bring up a touchy issue, I try to change the subject.

T F **4.** When it comes to dealing with difficult subjects, sometimes I steer the conversation to safer issues rather than address what really concerns me.

T F **5.** At times I avoid situations that might bring me into contact with people I'm having problems with.

T F **6.** I put off getting back to people sometimes because I'm uncomfortable dealing with them.

T F **7.** In order to get my point across, I sometimes exaggerate my side of the argument.

T F **8.** If I seem to be losing control of a conversation, I sometimes cut people off or change the subject to something that works better for me.

T F **9.** I suspect others walk away from conversations with me at times feeling belittled or hurt.

T F **10.** When I'm stunned by a comment, sometimes I say things that others might take as forceful or attacking— comments such as "Give me a break!" or "That's ridiculous!"

T F **11.** Sometimes when things get heated, I move from arguing against others' points to saying things that might hurt them personally.

T F **12.** When I feel threatened or hurt, I sometimes behave in ways that appear spiteful or vengeful.

T F **13.** I sometimes find myself having the same conversation with the same person multiple times.

T F **14.** At times I walk away from conversations with an agreement that I don't think really solves the problem.

T F **15.** When I'm discussing an important topic with others, sometimes I move from trying to make my point to trying to win the battle.

T F **16.** Sometimes I decide that it's better to keep the peace than share my views.

T F **17.** When talking about sensitive subjects, my emotions often get the best of me.

T F **18.** I sometimes walk away from conversations rehashing the reasons I'm right and others are wrong.

T F **19.** In the middle of a tough conversation, I often get so caught up in arguments that I don't see how I'm coming across to others.

T F **20.** When conversations start to deteriorate, I find it hard to figure out what's going wrong and get it back on track.

T F **21.** When I finally say what I really think, I tend to do so in a way that makes others feel defensive.

T F **22.** I often struggle to decide whether it's more important to say what I think or preserve the relationship.

T F **23.** Sometimes when I feel strongly about something, I say it in a way that others tend to resist.

T F **24.** When I am very confident of my opinion, I don't like it when others push back.

T F **25.** I'm often unsure of how to help others open up about things they are reluctant to share.

T F **26.** I spend more of my energy thinking about how to get my point across than worrying about how to help others express theirs.

T F **27.** I spend lots of time feeling very anxious when I'm facing a conversation where I think I might get tough feedback.

T F **28.** I can feel hurt and angry for a long time after a conversation where others said hurtful things to me.

T F **29.** I often have problems with people failing to do what we agreed to, and then the burden is on me to bring it up again.

T F **30.** When resolving tough things, we sometimes have clashing expectations about how the decision will be made, or even about what we agreed to when we talked.

STYLE UNDER STRESS TEST ONLINE

For quick scoring or to take the test again with different conversations in mind, visit crucialconversations.com. Your results will be generated automatically so you can see your typical tactics in Crucial Conversations. The results will also show you which chapters of this book might be most helpful to you.

Style Under Stress Score

Please fill out the score sheets in Figures 6.1 and 6.2. Each domain contains two checkboxes corresponding to two questions on the test. Give yourself a tick mark for any question you answered with a "T." If you answered "F," leave the tick box empty. Add up the total number of tick marks you have under Silence and the total you have under Violence in Figure 6.1 and enter the totals in the respective Silence and Violence boxes at the top of the columns. Do the same for the Dialogue Skill boxes in Figure 6.2. For example, count how many items you ticked in "Choose Your Topic" and enter that number in the box for that skill.

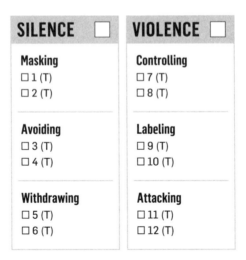

Figure 6.1　Style Under Stress score

Ch 3: Choose Your Topic	Ch 8: STATE My Path
☐ 13 (T) ☐ 14 (T) ☐	☐ 23 (T) ☐ 24 (T) ☐
Ch 4: Start with Heart	Ch 9: Explore Others' Paths
☐ 15 (T) ☐ 16 (T) ☐	☐ 25 (T) ☐ 26 (T) ☐
Ch 5: Master My Stories	Ch 10: Retake Your Pen
☐ 17 (T) ☐ 18 (T) ☐	☐ 27 (T) ☐ 28 (T) ☐
Ch 6: Learn to Look	Ch 11: Move to Action
☐ 19 (T) ☐ 20 (T) ☐	☐ 29 (T) ☐ 30 (T) ☐
Ch 7: Make It Safe	
☐ 21 (T) ☐ 22 (T) ☐	

Figure 6.2   Dialogue Skills score

What Your Score Means

Your Style Under Stress score (Figure 6.1) will show you which forms of silence or violence you turn to most often. Your silence and violence scores give you a measure of how frequently you fall into these less-than-perfect strategies. It's actually possible to score high in both. A medium or high score (one or two checked boxes per domain) means you sometimes or frequently use this technique.

Your Dialogue Skills score (Figure 6.2) is organized by concept and chapter so you can decide which chapters in this book might benefit you the most. The nine domains reflect your skills in each of the corresponding skill chapters. If you score zero, you're doing well in this area—at least in the scenarios you had in mind when you answered the questions. Note that your answers might be different if you thought about a more challenging situation. If you score one or two, you may want to pay special attention to these chapters.

Your score doesn't represent an unalterable character trait or a genetic propensity. It's merely a measure of your behavior under the circumstances you thought about when you answered the questions. And no matter your score, you can change that. In fact, people who take this book seriously will practice the skills in each chapter, and eventually they will change. They also occasionally retake the test for especially challenging relationships they are facing. As they do so, they become more and more competent at applying the skills under more and more taxing situations. And as they do so, their lives change for the better.

Once you've taken the test yourself, you might want to ask people who know you well to take it with you in mind. Does your assessment of your Style Under Stress match how others see you? If not, pay attention to the discrepancies and watch for what others are seeing. Learning to be a good self-monitor may take some time.

LOOKING VIRTUALLY

For many of us, more and more of our conversations, even our Crucial Conversations, are happening virtually, mediated through technology. We're calling, texting, emailing, and videoconferencing more than ever. So how do you learn to look when you aren't face-to-face?

Learning to look for signs that safety is at risk in a virtual environment is not actually that different from doing so in a face-to-face environment. The very best communicators realize that, at its heart, learning to look is about expanding your data stream. You see more, and as well you understand more about what you see.

The obvious challenge with most virtual communication is that our data stream is severely limited. Much of what we see when we're talking with people is communicated through their nonverbals—things like their body language, their tone of voice, or where they're looking, for example. Those nonverbal signals are important indicators that help us make sense of what they're saying. When a conversation moves to the telephone or to email, our data stream becomes more like a data trickle.

The solution is always the same. A better data stream gives you more to see in a conversation. If you know you need to have a Crucial Conversation, choose the medium that will give you the most band-width. For many, this is a face-to-face conversation. When that isn't possible, we often go next to videoconferencing and then a phone call. Eventually, we get to email, text, and instant messaging. With each step, we know we are decreasing the data available to us. It's not ideal, but when is real life ideal?

In real life, people manage teams on the other side of the world. Aging parents live far away. Teenagers ignore your call but moments later respond to a text ("Aha! I knew you were looking right at your phone when my call came in!"). Crucial Conversations happen virtually every day. And when they do, the goal is always the same. Expand the data stream. Learn to look for signs that safety is at risk.

How do you expand your data stream? Start by asking for more data. For example:

- **Email.** "I haven't heard back from you in a couple of days in response to the email I sent you. I am not sure how to interpret your silence. How are you feeling about the proposal?"
- **Telephone.** "I wish I could see your face right now. I don't know how you're hearing my message, and I would hate for you to misinterpret it. Can you help me understand what you're thinking right now?"
- **Direct messaging.** "When I read the comment that you posted on my social media account, I wasn't sure how to take it. It seemed like you might be upset. Are you?"

When you see signs of silence or violence in virtual communication, ask for more data. When you do, either people will add meaning to the pool about what they're feeling or thinking, or they'll hold back. If they don't disclose more about how they're feeling, that is its own confirming data. Then it's time to Make It Safe—the topic of the next chapter.

My Crucial Conversation: Tom E.

I am 55 years old, and we all know the saying: "You can't teach an old dog new tricks." I've worked in engineering and purchasing at the same company for 17 years. Throughout my career I've faced recurring interpersonal conflicts that resulted from frequent "blowups." I'd always believed that completing the task was the most important thing and that relationship damage was collateral damage I could live with.

My immediate superior had attended a Crucial Conversations class for the upper-level managers at our company. The next step was to enroll the next level of managers and coaches. I don't coach anyone, but my supervisor enrolled me in the class anyway.

My initial thought was, "I really don't have the time for this stuff!" But after the first few minutes, I realized that not only was I in the right place, but there was potential to learn something. I sat intently and absorbed as much as I could. As I "Learned to Look," I replayed past incidents in my mind and saw where I had gone wrong. I realized I paid no attention when interacting with others. I didn't notice when they went to silence or violence. It was "my way or the highway," and I would push until others went to silence, which to me signaled agreement.

During the training, I reread chapters and talked with classmates. I met with my learning partner, and he candidly told me that many of my coworkers believed I had a wealth of knowledge but avoided dealing with me because they didn't know when my next blowup would happen.

Shortly after I completed the class, the director of engineering called me into his office. He placed me on probation because of feedback about my blowups. I had three months to turn things around or I was gone. I thought overnight about what I was going to do. I realized that what I had learned about myself in the Crucial Conversations class gave me the tools to fix the problem. Prior to the class, I had no clue about how to turn things around and most likely would have walked out the door. Because of Crucial Conversations, however, I accepted the challenge.

My coach told me this would have to be a "life change" and not a temporary change, and I realized I had some fences to mend within the organization. I knew the road was going to be long and hard. Apologizing was difficult, but I wanted to change myself.

It is now a year later, and I still work for the same company. The things that have happened in the last year amaze me. I have mended all the fences, and at times, individuals have come to *me* for advice on dealing with situations. I have even had Crucial Conversations with managers of our company on behalf of others. My wife tells me the pattern of behavior of the last 30 years has changed. Things that used to cause me to blow up at home no longer do, and she says it's like being married to a different person. I am a different person—one even I like. Crucial Conversations has definitely changed me, and this old dog *has* learned new tricks.

SUMMARY: LEARN TO LOOK

When caught up in a Crucial Conversation, it's difficult to see exactly what's going on and why. When a discussion becomes stressful, we often end up doing the exact opposite of what works. We turn to the less healthy components of our Style Under Stress. To break from this insidious pattern, Learn to Look:

- At content *and* conditions
- For when things become crucial
- For safety problems
- To see if others are moving toward silence or violence
- For outbreaks of your Style Under Stress

7

MAKE IT SAFE

How to Make It Safe to Talk About Almost Anything

The last chapter contained a promise: If you spot safety risks as they happen, you can step out of the conversation, *build safety*, and then find a way to talk just about anything with just about anyone. In this chapter, we'll fulfill that promise by teaching what it takes to create and restore safety.

To get started, let's eavesdrop on a Crucial Conversation between a couple named Oba and Mari. Oba is a chef, and Mari is a project manager for a global supply chain company. The last year has been hard. A recession triggered a restructuring in Mari's company, and she was asked to take on additional responsibilities while downsizing her team. Worse, the restaurant Oba worked for closed, and he hasn't found another steady job. The financial strain of losing Oba's income compounded by the longer hours Mari is working has put an incredible amount of pressure on the relationship.

Oba feels that Mari doesn't have time for him or their relationship, that he is always coming second to work. Mari is feeling burned out from work and doesn't think Oba has picked up enough of the home responsibilities. For months, the two have been acting out their concerns rather than talking them out. When Mari works late, Oba feels rejected and pouts, sitting at home and watching television. Mari comes home, sees Oba sitting on the couch while the laundry still isn't done and dishes are piled in the sink. She gets angry, makes a snide remark, which makes Oba feel even more resentful. Mari retreats to their room, collapses exhausted onto the bed, and Oba eventually falls asleep on the couch.

After months of this, Oba decides to broach the topic with Mari. Rather than waiting to talk when they are both tired or upset, he picks a rare Sunday morning when they are having a relaxing brunch.

Oba: *Mari, I was wondering if we could talk about what happened on Friday night—you know, when you got home late from work and went straight to our room?*

Mari: *Oh, you mean Friday night when you were sitting on the couch rather than doing chores in the house? That Friday night?*

Oba: *Hey, I was waiting for you to get home so we could spend some time together.*

Mari: *Sure, you were waiting for me all right. Waiting for me to do everything around here that needs to be done. When are you going to start carrying your share of the load around here?*

Oba: *(Walks out.)*

STEP OUT. MAKE IT SAFE. THEN STEP BACK IN

OK, let's look at Oba. He tried to tackle a tough topic. Good for him. That wasn't easy after months of not saying anything, but he dove in anyway. And then his partner responded in a snarky way. Now what should he do? How can he get back to honest and healthy dialogue? What do you do when you don't feel safe sharing what's on your mind?

The key is to step out of the content of the conversation. That's right. When safety is at risk and you notice people moving to silence or violence, you need to step out of the content of the conversation (literally stop talking about the topic of your conversation) and rebuild safety. How do you do that?

You first need to understand why someone feels unsafe. People never become defensive about what you're saying (the content of your message). They become defensive because of why they think you're saying it (the intent). Said another way, safety in a conversation is about intent, not content. When people become defensive, it is because either:

1. You have a bad intent toward them (and they are accurately picking up on that).

Or:

2. They have misunderstood your good intent.

If it's the former, you need to go back and Start with Heart. Remember, it's easy for our motives to degrade in a Crucial Conversation. Check yourself by asking, what am I acting like I want? This question helps us see ourselves as other people are seeing us. Then ask yourself, what do you really want? For you? For them? For the relationship? If your motives have degraded, step back and refocus on what it is you really want.

Now, often the problem is not that we have a bad intent. It's that our intent has been misunderstood. Remember, human beings are wired to look for threats. When people feel threatened, they move to silence or verbal violence or to flight or fight—none of which are great for problem solving. All you need to do to destroy safety in a Crucial Conversation is . . . nothing. During these tense seconds at the beginning of a conversation, others are scanning your every facial tic or leg crossing for evidence of your intentions. Do you mean them harm? Are you out to get them? Your job is to generate evidence that that's not the case.

Take a moment to absorb that last sentence. It's not enough for you to have good intentions; the other person must know *that this is the case*. Think about this in the context of unconscious bias—the discomforts and judgments that we have about those who are different from us *and that we are unaware we carry*. These biases will cause you to communicate subtle signals to others that make them feel unsafe—breaking eye contact, stepping back a bit, frowning almost imperceptibly, etc. Similarly, they may carry unconscious biases toward you that make them feel less safe. This is one more reason to take on the task of generating clear and unmistakable evidence for them to the contrary.

In this case, Oba genuinely wanted to talk with Mari about their relationship. He loves her, and he knows that the way they have been treating each other isn't good for either of them. He wants to improve their relationship for both of them. So he speaks up, and Mari gets defensive. Why? Because she jumped to a conclusion about Oba's intent. Oba didn't provide any evidence at the outset of his intent, and so Mari probably (and predictably) thought he was attacking her (for the umpteenth time!) about the long hours she was working and how she never had time for him. Before he even finished his first sentence, she was on the defensive and she attacked back.

In these circumstances, the *worst* at dialogue do what Oba and Mari did. Like Mari, they say whatever is on their minds with no regard for how it will be received. Or like Oba, they conclude the topic is completely unsafe and move to silence.

Those who are *good* at dialogue realize that safety is at risk, but they fix it in exactly the wrong way. They try to make the subject more palatable by sugarcoating their message: "Oh, honey, I know you wanted to spend time together, but I was just so tired on Friday." They try to make things safer by watering down or dressing up their content. This strategy, of course, avoids the real problem, and it never gets fixed.

The *best* at dialogue don't play games. Period. They know that in order to solve their problem, they'll need to talk about their problem—with no pretending, sugarcoating, or faking. So they do something completely different. They step out of the content of the conversation, make it safe, and then step back in. Once safety is restored, they can talk about nearly anything.

TWO CONDITIONS OF SAFETY

In order for people to feel safe with you, they need to know two things about your intent. They need to know that:

- You care about their concerns (Mutual Purpose).
- You care about them (Mutual Respect).

We call Mutual Purpose and Mutual Respect the conditions of dialogue. Only when these two conditions are met, when there is Mutual Purpose and Mutual Respect, will you have the safety needed for meaning to flow into the pool. Let's look at each of these conditions in turn.

Mutual Purpose—the Entrance Condition

Remember the last time someone gave you difficult feedback and you didn't become defensive? Say a friend said some things to you that most people might get upset over. In order for this person to be able to deliver the delicate message, you must have believed he or she cared about you or about your goals and objectives. That means you trusted his or her *purposes* so you were willing to listen to some pretty tough feedback.

This is the first condition of safety—*Mutual Purpose*. Mutual Purpose means that others perceive that you're working toward a common outcome in the conversation, that you care about their goals, interests, and values. And vice versa. You believe they care about yours. Consequently, Mutual Purpose is the entry condition of dialogue. Find a shared goal, and you have both a good reason and a healthy climate for talking.

For example, if Mari believes that Oba's purpose in raising this delicate topic is to make her feel guilty or to get his way, this conversation is doomed from the outset. If she believes he really cares about making things better for both of them, he may have a chance.

A surefire Mutual Purpose. Sometimes it seems impossible to find a Mutual Purpose. You can't imagine any goal or purpose you and the other person could possibly have in common (after all, just think about whom he voted for in the last election! You'll never agree with this guy about anything!). But there is one way to always find Mutual Purpose in the conversation. You see, human beings have an innate need to be heard. We want to be listened to and understood. So a great Mutual Purpose to start with is to seek mutual understanding. If the other person truly believes you sincerely want to understand his or her needs or point of view, you have the basic makings of safety. And once the other person feels deeply understood, he or she is more likely to have the psychological resources to listen to you.

Remember the "mutual" in Mutual Purpose. There is a lot you can do in a conversation to create safety through Mutual Purpose. Later in this chapter, we'll lay out the specific steps you can take to create a Mutual Purpose when you find yourself at cross-purposes. But don't mistake your responsibility to create safety in the dialogue as meaning you should not expect the other person to acknowledge *your* needs. Mutual Purpose *must* be mutual. Yes, you need to care about the other person's purpose. But the other person also needs to care about your purpose. You don't need to subordinate your purpose to that of others just to create a veneer of safety for them.

So what do you do if the other person doesn't seem to care about your purpose? You choose *that* as the topic of the Crucial Conversation you need to have. After all, your purpose is every bit as important as the other person's, and you could and should hold that as a boundary. For example, you might say:

> *It's important to me that we have a collaborative and productive relationship. I'd like to talk about a pattern I've noticed in our conversations. I know we often have different goals or objectives. And I hope you know that I care about your objectives as well as my own. Sometimes, though, I sense that you don't really care about my goals, and that can make it tough for me to talk about things with you. I'm wondering if I've misread this.*

Look for the mutuality. Let's see how Mutual Purpose applies to a tough example—one where, at first glance, it might appear as if your purpose is to make things better for yourself. Let's say you've got a boss who frequently fails to keep commitments. How could you tell the boss you don't trust him? Surely there's no way to say this without him becoming defensive, right? Not necessarily.

To avoid disaster, find a Mutual Purpose that would be so motivating to the boss that he'd want to hear your concerns. If your only reason for approaching the boss is to get what you want, the boss will hear you as critical and selfish—which is what you are. In contrast, if you try to see the other person's point of view, you can often find a way to draw the person willingly into even very sensitive conversations. For example, if the boss's behavior is causing you to miss deadlines he cares about, or incur costs he frets over, or lose productivity he worries about, then you're onto a possible Mutual Purpose.

Imagine raising the topic this way: "I've got some ideas for how I can be much more reliable and even reduce costs by a few thousand dollars in preparing the report each month. It's going to be a bit of a sensitive conversation—but I think it will help a great deal if we can talk about it." Now you've got a *Mutual* Purpose.

Mutual Respect—the Continuance Condition

While it's true that there's no reason to enter a Crucial Conversation if you don't have Mutual Purpose, it's equally true that you can't stay in the conversation if you don't maintain *Mutual Respect.* Mutual Respect is the continuance condition of dialogue. As people perceive that others don't respect them, the conversation immediately becomes unsafe, and dialogue comes to a screeching halt.

Why? Because respect is like air. As long as it's present, nobody thinks about it. But if you take it away, it's *all* that people can think about. The instant people perceive disrespect in a conversation, the interaction is no longer about the original purpose—it is now about defending dignity.

For example, you're talking with a group of supervisors about a complicated quality problem. You really want to see the problem resolved once and for all. Your job depends on it. Unfortunately, you also think the supervisors are overpaid and underqualified. You firmly believe that not only are they in over their heads, but they do stupid things all the time. Some of them even act unethically.

As the supervisors throw out ideas, you roll your eyes. The disrespect you carry in your head creeps out in one unfortunate gesture, and now it's all over. Without Mutual Respect, the conversation tanks. The supervisors take shots at your proposals. You add insulting adjectives in describing theirs. As attention turns to scoring points, everyone loses. Your Mutual Purpose suffers from a lack of Mutual Respect.

Telltale signs. To spot when respect is violated and safety takes a turn south, watch for signs that people are defending their dignity. Emotions are the key. When people feel disrespected, they become highly charged.

Their emotions turn from fear to anger. Then they resort to pouting, name-calling, yelling, and making threats. To determine when Mutual Respect is at risk, ask yourself, "Do others believe I respect them?"

Can You Respect People You Don't Respect?

Some people fear they'll never be able to maintain Mutual Respect with certain individuals or in certain circumstances. How, they wonder, can I respect someone who behaves in ways I deplore? What do you do, for example, if you're upset because another person has let you down? And if this has repeatedly happened, how can you respect a person who is so poorly motivated and selfish?

Dialogue truly would be doomed if we had to respect every element of another person's character before we could talk. If this were the case, the only person we'd be able to talk to would be ourselves. However, we can stay in dialogue by finding a way to honor and regard another person's basic humanity. In essence, feelings of disrespect often come when we dwell on how others are *different* from ourselves. We can counteract these feelings by looking for ways we are similar. Without excusing others' behavior, we try to sympathize, even empathize, with them.

A rather clever person once hinted how to do this in the form of a prayer—"Lord, help me forgive those who sin *differently* than I." When we recognize that we all have weaknesses, it's easier to find a way to respect others. When we do this, we feel a kinship between ourselves and even the thorniest of people. This connection to others helps create Mutual Respect and eventually enables us to stay in dialogue with virtually anyone.

Consider the following true example. Workers at a manufacturing company had been out on strike for over six months. Finally, the union agreed to return to work, but the represented employees had to sign a contract that was worse than what they were originally demanding. On the first day back, it was clear that although people would work, they wouldn't do so with a smile and a spring in their step. Everyone was furious. How were people ever going to move ahead?

Concerned that although the strike was over, the battle wasn't, a manager asked one of the authors to lend a hand. The author met with the two groups of leaders (both managers and union heads) and asked them to do one thing. Each group was to go into a separate room and write out its goals for the company on flip-chart–sized paper. For two hours, each group feverishly laid out what it wanted in the future and then taped the lists to the wall. When they finished their assignment, the groups were asked to swap places with the goal of finding something—anything—they might have in common.

After a few minutes, the two groups returned to the training room. They were positively stunned. It was as if they had written the exact same lists. They didn't merely share the shadow of an idea or two. Their aspirations were nearly identical. All wanted a profitable company, stable and rewarding jobs, high-quality products, and a positive impact on the community. Given a chance to speak freely and without fear of attack, each group laid out not simply what *it* wanted, but what virtually every person wanted.

This experience caused members from each group to seriously question how they had judged the other side. They began to see others as more similar to themselves. They realized the petty and political tactics the others had used were embarrassingly similar to the ones they themselves had employed. The "sins" of others were different from their own more because of the role they played than because of a fundamental blight on their character. They restored Mutual Respect, and dialogue replaced silence and violence for the first time in decades.

BUILD, AND REBUILD, SAFETY

We know we need to have both Mutual Purpose and Mutual Respect in order to have an effective dialogue.

We've also argued that you should be able to find a way to both find Mutual Purpose and enjoy Mutual Respect—even with people who are flawed or different.

But how? What are you supposed to actually do? Here are four skills that the *best* at dialogue routinely use to build safety up front in a conversation and rebuild safety when it's been lost:

- Share your good intent.
- Apologize when appropriate.
- Contrast to fix misunderstandings.
- Create a Mutual Purpose.

Share Your Good Intent

As we have discussed, if people aren't sure of your intent, they will assume the worst. We saw this with Oba and Mari. Oba opened the conversation with a seemingly innocuous statement: "Mari, I was wondering if we could talk about what happened on Friday night— you know, when you got home late from work and went straight to our room?"

He asked to talk and related the facts. And what happened? Mari immediately got defensive. Why? Because she assumed Oba was bringing up this topic so that he could criticize her for her behavior. And why wouldn't she when that's how he framed the conversation? He set the whole thing up as "Let's talk about you going straight into our room." It's no surprise that Mari felt unsafe.

But let's step back for a moment. If we asked Oba, "What do you really want here?," he would say, "I want a better relationship with Mari. I want to be honest with her about how I feel, and I want her to be honest with me. I want us to be gentle with each other as we talk about tough things."

So imagine if Oba started the conversation with that.

Oba: *Mari, I was wondering if we could talk about what happened on Friday night. I love you, and I want to make sure we're talking about things that impact our relationship, because our relationship is the most important thing in the world to me. I'm sure there are things you'd like me to change, and I want to understand those as well as share concerns I have. Could we talk?*

When you start the conversation by sharing your good intent, you lay the foundation for safety. It doesn't mean that the other person won't get defensive as the conversation progresses, but it does give you the touchstone you need to return to again and again when safety is at risk.

Apologize When Appropriate

When you've made a mistake that has hurt others, start with an apology. An apology is a statement that sincerely expresses your sorrow for your role in causing—or at least not preventing—pain or difficulty to others.

For example, the division vice president is coming to your plant for a tour. Part of the tour includes a visit with the members of the quality team, who have recently put some new process improvements in place. The team members are excited and have worked all night prepping for the VIP tour. Unfortunately, when it comes time to swing by their area, the visiting VP drops a bomb. He lays out a new production plan that you're convinced will hurt quality and potentially drive away your biggest customers. Since you only have another hour with the VP, you choose to talk through the issue rather than conduct the tour. Your future depends on this particular conversation. Fortunately, you and the VP are able to come to agreement on a new plan. Unfortunately, you forgot to get word to the team that had worked so hard.

As you walk back to your office after escorting the executive to her car, you bump into the team. Bleary-eyed and disappointed, all six team members are fuming. No visit, no phone call, and now it's clear from the way you were sprinting past them that you weren't even going to stop and offer a simple explanation.

Ouch.

Things start turning ugly: "We pulled an all-nighter, and you didn't even bother to come by! Not even a text message to tell us something came up. Thanks a lot."

Time stands still. This conversation has just turned crucial. The employees who worked so hard are obviously upset. They feel disrespected—despite the fact that you weren't trying to be disrespectful.

But you fail to restore safety. Why? Because now *you* feel disrespected. They've attacked you. So you stay stuck in the content of the conversation, thinking this has something to do with the factory tour: "I had to choose between the future of the company and a facility tour. I chose our future, and I'd do it again if I had to."

Now both you and they are fighting for respect. This is getting you nowhere fast. But what else can you do?

Instead of getting hooked and fighting back, break the cycle. See their aggressive behavior for what it is—a sign of violated safety—then step out of the conversation and rebuild safety by restoring respect. It's time to apologize sincerely for being disrespectful: "I'm sorry I didn't give you a call when I learned that we wouldn't be coming by. You worked all night. It would have been a wonderful chance to showcase your improvements, and I didn't even explain to you what happened. I apologize."

Now an apology isn't really an apology unless you experience a change in heart. To offer a sincere apology, your motives have to change. You have to give up saving face, being right, or winning in order to focus on what you *really* want. You have to sacrifice a bit of your ego by admitting your error. But like many sacrifices, when you give up something you value, you're rewarded with something even more valuable—healthy dialogue and better results.

Contrast to Fix Misunderstandings

Sometimes others feel disrespected during Crucial Conversations even though you haven't done anything disrespectful. Sure, there are times when respect gets violated because you behave in clearly hurtful ways. But just as often, the insult is entirely unintended.

The same can happen with Mutual Purpose. You can start by innocently sharing your views, but other people believe your intention is to harm them or coerce them into accepting your opinion. Clearly an apology is not appropriate in these circumstances. It would be disingenuous to admit you were wrong when you weren't. How, then, can you rebuild Mutual Purpose or Mutual Respect in order to make it safe to get back to dialogue?

When others misinterpret either your purpose or your intent, step out of the argument and rebuild safety by using a skill called "Contrasting."

Contrasting is a don't/do statement that fixes misunderstandings:

- In the "don't" part of the statement, you explain what you don't intend for the conversation. This addresses others' concerns that you don't respect them or that you have a malicious purpose.
- In the "do" part of the statement, you clarify what your intention for the conversation really is. This confirms your respect or clarifies your real purpose.

For example, with Oba and Mari:

Mari (defensively): *Why are you always on my case? I'm working as hard as I can and carrying this huge load while you watch TV!*

Oba (using Contrasting to restore purpose): *I don't want to criticize you or get on your case. That wasn't my intent, and I know you're carrying a huge load. I do want us to be able to* *talk about our concerns with each other so we can address them and build our relationship.*

Or with the you and the quality team after the VP's nonvisit:

Team (defensively): *You totally ignored us and the work we've done to make this plant run!*

You (using Contrasting to restore respect): *The last thing I wanted to do was communicate that I don't value the work you put in or that I don't want to share it with the VP. I think your work has been nothing short of amazing, and I am committed to making sure the VP knows that.*

Of the two parts of Contrasting, the *don't* is the more important because it deals with the misunderstanding that has put safety at risk. The employees who worked so hard are acting on the belief that you don't appreciate their efforts and didn't care enough to keep them informed—when the exact opposite was true. When people misunderstand and you start arguing over the misunderstanding, stop. Use Contrasting. Explain what you don't mean until you've restored safety. Then return to the conversation. Safety first.

Once you've done this and safety returns to the conversation, then you can explain what you do intend. Safety first.

Use Contrasting to provide context and proportion. When you're in the middle of a touchy conversation, sometimes others experience your words as bigger or worse than you intend. For example, you talk with your assistant about his lack of punctuality. When you share your concern, he appears crushed.

At this point, you could be tempted to water down your content—"You know it's really not that big a deal." Don't give in to the temptation. Don't take back what you've said, and don't apologize for it. Instead, put your remarks in context. For instance, at this point your assistant may believe you are completely dissatisfied with his performance. He believes that your view of the issue at hand represents the totality of your respect for him. If this belief is incorrect, use Contrasting to clarify what you don't and do believe. Start with what you don't believe:

> **What you don't believe:** *"Let me put this in perspective. I don't want you to think I'm not satisfied with the quality of your work. I want us to continue working together. I really do think you're doing a good job."*

> **What you do believe:** *"This punctuality issue is important to me, and I'd just like you to work on that. If you will be more attentive to that, there are no other issues."*

Use Contrasting for prevention. So far we've shown how Contrasting can be used as first aid for a wounded conversation. Someone has taken something wrong, and we've intervened to clarify our true purpose or meaning. However, Contrasting can also be a powerful tool for preventing safety problems. In this respect, it's similar to starting a conversation by sharing your good intent. Two examples:

> *"I wanted to talk about how we're managing our finances. I don't want you to think that I don't appreciate the time you've taken to keep our checking account balanced and up to date. I do appreciate it, and I know I certainly couldn't have done nearly as well. I do, however, have some concerns with how we're using the new online banking system."*

> *"I'd like to talk to you about something that's worrying me, and I'm honestly not sure how to handle this conversation.*

My fear is that I'll draw down on our relationship, and that's not my intent at all. It's the opposite. My goal in bringing this up is to strengthen our relationship."

Contrasting for prevention of safety problems works well when you have some experience with the other person and have a good guess, based on that experience, of how the person may misunderstand your intent.

Create a Mutual Purpose

Sometimes we find ourselves in the middle of a debate because we clearly have different purposes. There is no misunderstanding here. Contrasting won't do the trick. We need something sturdier for this job.

For instance, you've just been offered a promotion that will help propel your career along a faster track and bring you a great deal more authority. And it pays enough to help soften the blow of displacement. That last part is important because you'll have to move the family across the country, and your spouse and kids love where you currently live.

You expected your spouse to have feelings of *ambivalence* over the move, but he or she doesn't seem to be ambivalent even a tiny bit. To your spouse, the promotion is a bad news/bad news event. First, you have to move, and second, you'll work even longer hours. That whole thing about more money and power doesn't seem to be compensating for the loss of time together. Now what?

The *worst* at dialogue either ignore the problem and push ahead or roll over and let others have their way. They opt for either competition or submission. Both strategies end up making winners and losers, and the problem continues long beyond the initial conversation.

The *good* at dialogue move immediately toward compromise. For example, the couple facing the transfer sets up two households—one where the transferred spouse will be working and one where the family currently lives. Nobody really wants this arrangement, and frankly, it's a pretty ugly solution that's bound to lead to more serious problems, even divorce. While compromise is sometimes necessary, the *best* know better than to start there.

The *best* at dialogue use four skills to create a Mutual Purpose. If it helps you remember what to do, note that the four skills used in creating Mutual Purpose form the acronym CRIB.

Commit to Seek Mutual Purpose

As with most dialogue skills, if we want to get back to dialogue, we have to Start with Heart. In this case, we have to *agree to agree*. To be successful, we have to stop using silence or violence to compel others to our view. We must even surrender false dialogue, where we pretend to have Mutual Purpose (calmly arguing our side until the other person gives in). We Start with Heart by committing to stay in the conversation until we invent a solution that serves a purpose we both share.

This can be tough. To stop arguing, we have to suspend our belief that our choice is the absolute best and only one, and that we'll never be happy until we get exactly what we currently want. We have to open our mind to the fact that maybe, just maybe, there is a third choice out there—one that suits everyone.

We also have to be willing to verbalize this commitment even when our partner seems committed to winning. We act on faith that our partner is stuck in silence or violence because he or she feels unsafe. We assume that if we build more safety—by demonstrating our commitment to finding a Mutual Purpose—the other person will feel more confident that dialogue could be a productive avenue.

So next time you find yourself stuck in a battle of wills, try this amazingly powerful but simple skill: Step out of the content of the struggle and make it safe. Simply say: "It seems like we're both trying to force our view on each other. I commit to stay in this discussion until we have a solution that satisfies both of us." Then watch whether safety takes a turn for the better.

Recognize the Purpose Behind the Strategy

Wanting to come up with a shared goal is a wonderful first step, but desire alone is not enough. After we've experienced a change of heart, we need to change our strategy as well. Here's the problem we have to fix: When we find ourselves at an impasse, it's because we're asking for one thing and the other person is asking for something else. We think we'll never find a way out because we equate what we're asking for with what we actually want. In truth, what we're asking for is the *strategy* we're suggesting to get what we want. We confuse wants or purpose with strategies. That's the problem.

For example, I come home from work and say that I want to go to a movie. You say that you want to stay home and relax. And so we debate: movie, TV, movie, read, etc. We figure we'll never be able to resolve our differences because going out and staying home are incompatible.

In such circumstances, we can break the impasse by asking others, "Why do you want that?" In the above case, it might go like this:

"Why do you want to stay home?"

"Because I'm tired of running around and dealing with the hassle of the city."

"So you want peace and quiet?"

"Mostly. And why do you want to go to a movie?"

"So I can spend some time with you away from the kids."

Before you can agree on a Mutual Purpose, you must first know what people's real purposes are. Step out of the content of the conversation—which is generally focused on strategies—and explore the purposes behind them.

When you do separate strategies from purpose, new options become possible. By releasing your grip on your strategy and focusing on your real purpose, you're now open to the idea that you might actually find alternatives that can serve both of your interests:

> *"You want peace and quiet, and I want time with you away from the kids. So if we can come up with something that is quiet and away, we'll both be happy. Is that right?"*

> *"Absolutely. What if we were to take a drive up the canyon and..."*

Invent a Mutual Purpose

Sometimes when you recognize the purposes behind another person's strategies, you discover that you actually have compatible goals. From there you simply come up with common strategies. But you're not always so lucky. For example, you find out that your genuine wants and goals cannot be served except at the expense of the other person's. In this case you cannot *discover* a Mutual Purpose. That means you'll have to actively *invent* one.

To invent a Mutual Purpose, move to more encompassing goals. Find an objective that is more meaningful or more rewarding than the ones that divide the various sides. For instance, you and your spouse may not agree on whether or not you should take the promotion, but you can agree that the needs of your relationship and the children come before career aspirations. By focusing on higher and longer-term goals, you often find ways to transcend short-term compromises, build Mutual Purpose, and return to dialogue.

Brainstorm New Strategies

Once you've built safety by finding a shared purpose, you should have enough safety to return to the content of the conversation. It's time to step back into the dialogue and brainstorm strategies that meet everyone's needs. If you've committed to finding something everyone can support and you've surfaced what you really want, you'll no longer be spending your energy on unproductive conflict. Instead, you'll be actively coming up with options that can serve everyone.

Suspend judgment and think outside the box for new alternatives. Can you find a way to work in a job that is local and still meets your career goals? Is *this* job with *this* company the only thing that will make you happy? Is a move really necessary in this new job? Is there another community that could offer your family the same benefits? If you're not willing to give creativity a try, it'll be impossible for you to jointly come up with a mutually acceptable option. On the other hand, if you are able to, the sky's the limit.

Create a Mutual Purpose

In summary, when you sense that you and others are working at cross-purposes, here's what you can do. First, step out of the content of the conflict. Stop focusing on who thinks what. Then create a Mutual Purpose:

- **Commit to seek a Mutual Purpose.** Make a unilateral public commitment to stay in the conversation until you come up with something that serves everyone.

  "This isn't working. Your team is arguing to stay late and work until we're done, and my team wants to go home and come back on the weekend. Why don't we see if we can come up with something that satisfies everyone?"

- **Recognize the purpose behind the strategy.** Ask people why they want what they're pushing for. Separate what they're demanding from the purpose it serves.

  "Exactly why don't you want to come in Saturday morning? We're feeling fatigued and are worried about safety issues and a loss of quality. Why do you want to stay late?"

- **Invent a Mutual Purpose.** If after clarifying everyone's purposes you're still at odds, see if you can invent a higher or longer-term purpose that's more motivating than the ones that keep you in conflict.

  "I certainly don't want to make winners and losers here. It's far better if we can come up with something that doesn't make one team resent the other. We've voted before or flipped a coin, and the losers just ended up resenting the winners. I'm more worried about how we feel about each other than anything else. Let's make sure that whatever we do, we don't drive a wedge into our working relationship."

- **Brainstorm new strategies.** With a clear Mutual Purpose, you can join forces in searching for a solution that serves everyone.

  "So we need to come up with something that doesn't jeopardize safety and quality and allows your team to attend your colleague's wedding on Saturday afternoon. My team members have a game Saturday morning. What if your team were to work the morning and early afternoon, and then our team can come in after the game and take over from there? That way we'll be able . . ."

WRITE IT TWICE

Thus far, we've been sharing examples of how to create or restore safety in a conversation that's happening face-to-face (in person or online) or, at the very least, on the phone. But what about safety in written communication like email or text?

Well, hold on to your seats for this one . . . because it turns out that you create safety in written communication the same way you do in face-to-face conversation. Yep, if you are emailing another human being and want to create safety for the person, the key is to remember that you are emailing another human being. And then create safety by sharing your good intent, because that's what makes it safe for human beings. Revolutionary, we know.

The core conditions of safety don't change based on the medium. If I know you care about me (Mutual Respect) and I know you care about what I care about (Mutual Purpose), I'll feel safe with you, whether conversing face-to-face or reading an email. The key difference in email and other written communication is that it is even *more* essential to verbalize your good intent.

In face-to-face conversation, we share our intent with both words (we apologize, contrast, etc.) and nonverbals (our tone of voice, our body language, eye contact, etc.). When visual cues are removed, it becomes even more essential to use our words to communicate our intent.

Problematically, at the moment that it's most important to remember, we forget that we're communicating with a human being who needs to feel safe. After all, no one else is around. It's just us and our keyboard, and we are typing away.

So here's a tip for making sure you communicate intent when typing a crucial message to someone: Write it twice. First, write the message to get your content across. Once you have your content down, consider how your intent is coming across. Read the message slowly, imagining the other person's face. How might the person feel at each point in your message? Then rewrite it with safety in mind. Notice places someone may misunderstand your intentions or your respect, and clarify what you do and don't intend for them to hear. In less formal, more personal relationships, you may even want to describe the facial expression you're wearing as you write something just to make your intent even clearer. For example, "If you could see my face right now as I write this, you'd probably see the wrinkles in my worried forehead as I hope that my message isn't coming across as harsh or critical."

We tend to think of asynchronous, written communication as a distant second-best when it comes to having Crucial Conversations.

And in most ways, it is. However, there is one advantage to asynchronous communication if you are savvy enough to use it. With virtual communication, like email, you get your second chance before you need it, before you even messed up. Rather than saying something and then thinking, "I could have said that better," you get to write something and then reread it before you ever send it. We have to learn the discipline of taking that second chance to build safety before we need it.

 ## HOW DO I HAVE A CRUCIAL CONVERSATION VIRTUALLY?

Virtual conversations—whether they take place via videoconferencing, text, or phone call—bring a different dynamic to a Crucial Conversation. Coauthor Emily Gregory shares tips on how you can tee up a virtual Crucial Conversation for success. See the video *How Do I Have a Crucial Conversation Virtually?* at crucialconversations.com.

BACK TO OBA AND MARI

Let's end the chapter where we started. Oba is going to try to move to dialogue with Mari. Let's see how he does at making it safe in this Crucial Conversation. Because they have tried to have this conversation before and failed, he has a good idea of how Mari might misunderstand his intent. So he'll start by sharing his good intent with a Contrasting statement.

> **Oba:** *Mari, I'd like to talk about how much you're working and how it's impacting our relationship. I'm not bringing this up to criticize you or suggest the problem is yours. I know you're under tremendous pressure at work right now, and I am so*

*grateful for the sacrifices you're making for our family. I really
just want to talk about what we can do to make things better
for both of us in this new reality we're in.*

Mari: *What's there to talk about? I work. You don't. I am trying
to accept that.*

Oba: *I think it's more complicated than that. And when you
say things like that, it makes me wonder if you respect me
anymore.*

Mari: *If that's how you feel, why are we pretending we have a
relationship at all?*

OK, what just happened? Remember, we're exploring Oba's side
of the conversation. He's the one initiating the talk. Clearly there's a lot
Mari could be doing to make things go better. But what should Oba do if
he wants the conversation to go better? He should stay focused on what
he really wants: to find a way to make things better for both of them.
Consequently, he shouldn't respond to the content of Mari's discourag-
ing statement. Rather, he should look at the safety issue behind it. Why
is Mari starting to withdraw from the conversation? Two reasons:

- The way Oba made his point sounded to her like he was blaming
  her for everything.
- She believes his concern in one small area reflects his total
  feelings toward her.

So he'll apologize and use Contrasting to rebuild safety.

Oba: *I'm sorry I said it that way. I'm not blaming you for how I
feel or act. That's my problem. I don't see this as your problem.
I see it as our problem. Both of us may be acting in ways that
make things worse. I know I am, at least.*

Mari: *I probably am, too. Sometimes I pout because I'm just so overwhelmed and burned out. And I also do it hoping it'll make you feel bad. I'm sorry about that, too.*

Notice what just happened. Since Oba dealt well with the safety issue and kept focused on what he really wanted out of this conversation, Mari returned to the conversation. This is far more effective than if Oba had gone into blaming.

Let's continue.

Mari: *I just don't see how we can work this out. My job is what it is right now. With you out of work, I'm not really in a position to cut back or try to renegotiate. And when I come home and see all the housework that hasn't been done, it's just really frustrating. I know you want us to spend more time together, but I'm exhausted and need time on my own to recharge.*

The problem now is one of Mutual Purpose. Mari thinks she and Oba are at cross-purposes. In her mind, there is no possibility of a mutually satisfactory solution. She only has 24 hours in the day. Rather than move to compromise or fight for his way, Oba will step out of the issue and use CRIB to get to Mutual Purpose.

Oba: (**C**ommit to seek Mutual Purpose.) *I know you're stretched thin, and I don't want something that doesn't work for you. I want to find a way to have us both feel close, appreciated, and loved.*

Mari: *That's what I want, too. It just seems like there is not enough time in the day for that.*

Oba: (**R**ecognize the purpose behind the strategy.) *Maybe, but maybe not. What would make you feel loved and appreciated in our relationship?*

Mari: *Well, it's hard to say this because I don't want to hurt you and I know this is sensitive. . . . I know you feel bad about being out of work. I get that. But you are out of work right now. And it would really help me feel better about our relationship if you started to take on more of the work at home, like the dishes and laundry and stuff. When we were both working, we divided that 50-50, but we're not both working now.*

Oba: *OK. That's fair. And I'm glad you said that. I have struggled with a lot of self-doubt, and it has really impacted my motivation. I think that's one of the reasons that now, maybe more than ever, I'm really craving time with you, just fun time where we can talk and laugh and enjoy each other's company.*

Mari: *I get that. But it's hard to enjoy anything when I'm so burned out. And then I resent you for the pressure I feel.*

Oba: *Yep. I hear that. And I feel that resentment, which just makes me feel even worse about myself, because I know I'm letting you down.*

Mari: (**I**nvent a Mutual Purpose.) *So we need to find some ways to get some of the load off my shoulders so that we can enjoy each other more. I really want that, too, you know.*

Oba: *I know you do. I don't imagine either of us likes feeling this way.*

Mari: (**B**rainstorm new strategies.) *Well, what if we . . .*

Oba and Mari haven't solved their problem yet, and there are a lot of real-world constraints that will make it difficult. However, they are far more likely to solve their problem and build their relationship than they were at the beginning of this chapter. Creating safety doesn't resolve all our issues; it simply creates the space to give dialogue a chance.

My Crucial Conversation: Dr. Jerry M.

On a Monday, a woman was admitted to my hospital for same-day vascular bypass surgery to repair a painful extremity below the knee that wasn't adequately circulating blood. She lived in Mississippi and had traveled two hours to Memphis to see a doctor. The surgeon skillfully performed the procedure, and the outcome was excellent. The next day, the patient and her husband were deliriously happy because the terrible pain in her foot was gone.

The case manager and physician had tentatively agreed that if everything was fine, the patient could be discharged Thursday afternoon. As the patient continued to improve, the case manager made arrangements for a Thursday discharge.

On Thursday morning, the case manager told the patient's husband to come and pick up his wife, unaware that the doctor had written the following note: *Patient doing fine, foot warm, pulse excellent, patient stable. Plan: Discharge Friday a.m.*

Seeing the note, the case manager attempted to reach the surgeon and finally contacted him late that afternoon as he frantically rushed to his office. Running late, the surgeon bluntly said, "I need to see this patient before discharge. I won't be in until tomorrow. The patient is not going home today, and that's that."

Around 3:00 p.m., the case manager contacted me for help. I immediately called the surgeon and began our conversation by praising his success and offering my assistance. I explained that the patient's family had driven two hours to pick her up and she was ready to go.

I offered to do the paperwork while he gave instructions to the couple over the phone, but he persisted, "No. I need to see this patient, and I can't be in until tomorrow." And then defensively he raised his voice, "Is the insurance company putting you up to this? I mean, why are you pressuring me?"

Taken aback, I responded by using the Contrasting skill: "Honestly, I don't even know who the payer is. This isn't about the insurance company; this is about meeting the needs of the patient and the family. They've had a wonderful experience. They think you walk on water. They were told they could go home, and I'm afraid canceling the discharge could sully an otherwise wonderful clinical outcome."

Floundering a bit, the surgeon responded, "Tell them I'll be in, but it won't be until 7:00."

Reaching agreement, I promised to communicate his willingness to make a special trip back and personally give instructions. He came in that night, discharged the patient, and avoided tarnishing an otherwise excellent episode of care.

In the healthcare environment, Crucial Conversations are real, they're up front, and they happen all the time. This conversation was successful because I followed two of the quintessential rules: Mutual Respect and Mutual Purpose.

SUMMARY: MAKE IT SAFE

Step Out of the Content
When others move to silence or violence, step out of the content of the conversation and Make It Safe. When safety is restored, go back to the issue at hand and continue the dialogue.

Decide Which Condition of Safety Is at Risk
- **Mutual Purpose.** Do others believe you care about their goals in this conversation? Do they trust your motives?
- **Mutual Respect.** Do others believe you respect them?

Share Your Good Intent
To start the conversation off right, share your positive intent. What do you really want? For you and the other person.

Apologize When Appropriate
When you've clearly violated respect, apologize.

Contrast to Fix Misunderstanding
When others misunderstand either your purpose or your intent, use Contrasting. Start with what you don't intend or mean. Then explain what you do intend or mean.

Create a Mutual Purpose
When you are at cross-purposes, use the four CRIB skills to get back to Mutual Purpose:

- **C**ommit to seek Mutual Purpose.
- **R**ecognize the purpose behind the strategy.
- **I**nvent a Mutual Purpose.
- **B**rainstorm new strategies.

8

STATE MY PATH

How to Speak Persuasively, Not Abrasively

So far, we've gone to great pains to prepare ourselves to step up to and master Crucial Conversations. Here's what we've learned. Our hearts need to be in the right place, and our heads need to be focused on the right topic. We need to let go of the clever stories that are keeping us stuck. We need to learn to look closely at how people are engaging in the dialogue—particularly when people start feeling unsafe—so that we can restore safety when necessary.

So let's say that we are well prepared. We're ready to open our mouths and start sharing our point of view. That's right, we're actually going to express our opinion. Now what?

Most of the time, we walk into a discussion and slide into autopilot: "Hi, how are the kids? What's going on at work?" What could be easier than talking? We know thousands of words and generally weave them into sentences that suit our needs. Most of the time.

However, when both the stakes and our emotions rise, well, that's when we open our mouths and don't do so well. In fact, as we suggested earlier, the more important the discussion, the less likely we are to be on our best behavior. Sadly, as we'll see, we express our views in a way that is perfectly designed to provoke defensiveness.

To help us improve our advocacy skills, we'll examine five skills that solve our two main problems: defensiveness and resistance. First, we'll look at how the five skills help you design your message in a way that helps others to hear it. And second, we'll explore how these same skills help you be more persuasive at times when your own certainty is your worst enemy.

SHARE RISKY MEANING

Adding information to the pool of meaning can be quite difficult when the ideas we're about to pour into the collective consciousness contain delicate, unattractive, or controversial opinions. As in: "Marta, people simply don't like working with you. I'm cutting you from the special-projects team."

It's one thing to argue that your company needs to shift from green to red packaging; it's quite another to tell a person that he or she is offensive or unlikable. When the topic turns from things to people, it's always more difficult. To nobody's surprise, some people are better at approaching these conversations than others.

When it comes to sharing touchy information, the *worst* alternate between bluntly dumping their ideas into the pool of meaning and saying nothing at all. Either they start with, "You're not going to like this, but, hey, somebody has to be honest . . ." (a classic Fool's Choice), or they simply stay quiet.

Those who are *good* at dialogue say some of what's on their minds, but they understate their views out of fear of hurting others. They talk all right, but they carefully sugarcoat their message. For example, rather than being honest that they think your marketing piece will be an embarrassment to the company, they say: "Uh, well, I like the graphics a lot. But I think we can spice up the text a little here and there."

The *best* at dialogue speak their minds completely and do it in a way that makes it safe for others to hear what they have to say and respond to it as well. They are both totally candid and completely respectful. If they think the marketing piece is bad, they make sure when they are done that you know they think the marketing piece is bad. But they do so in a way that is 100 percent respectful as well.

How? By finding a way to maintain safety *without* compromising candor.

MAINTAIN SAFETY

In order to speak honestly when honesty could easily offend others, we have to find a way to maintain safety. That's a bit like telling someone to smash another person in the nose, but, you know, don't hurt him. How can we speak the unspeakable and still maintain respect? It can be done if you know how to carefully blend three ingredients: confidence, humility, and skill.

Confidence. Most people simply won't hold delicate conversations—well, at least not with the right person. For instance, your colleague Brian goes home at night and tells his wife that his boss, Fernando, is micromanaging him to within an inch of his life. He says the same thing over lunch when talking with his pals. Everyone knows what Brian thinks about Fernando—except, of course, Fernando.

People who are skilled at dialogue have the confidence to say what needs to be said to the person who needs to hear it. They are confident that their opinions deserve to be placed in the pool of meaning. They are also confident that they can speak openly without brutalizing others or causing undue offense.

Humility. Confidence does not equate to arrogance or pigheadedness. Skilled people are confident that they have something to say, but also realize that others have valuable input. They realize that they don't have a monopoly on the truth. They are curious about information and perspectives others have. Their opinions provide a starting point but not the final word. They may currently believe something but realize that with new information they may change their minds. This means they're willing to both express their opinions and encourage others to do the same.

Skill. Finally, people who willingly share delicate information are good at doing it. That's why they're confident in the first place. They don't make a Fool's Choice, because they've found a path that allows for both candor and safety. They speak the unspeakable, and more often than you'd suspect, others are grateful for their honesty.

Skill comes from practice and repetition. Yes, reading this book and learning the skills of dialogue is an important first step. But reading alone won't make you better at dialogue. You have to start holding Crucial Conversations if you want to get better at holding Crucial Conversations.

The Missing Money

To see how to discuss sensitive issues, let's look at a difficult problem. Anita has just opened her wallet at the checkout stand. She reaches in to pull out the pair of twenties she is planning to use for the groceries she is buying. But wait. There is no money. She looks through the various compartments and still—no $20 bills. She immediately turns to her 16-year-old daughter standing next to her. Then Anita barks in a loud voice: "Amber! Where is it?"

Well, that was fast. It took Anita all of half a second to jump from "I thought I had $40 in here" to "She rifled through my wallet and took my cash!"

Now what's the worst way Anita might handle this (one that doesn't involve banishing her daughter to her bedroom with bread and water rations until she is 25)? What's the worst way of *talking* about the problem? Most people agree that jumping in with an ugly accusation followed by a threat is a good candidate for that distinction. It's also what most people do, and Anita is no exception.

"I can't believe you would steal from me! You want to spend the next decade in your room?" she says in an aggrieved tone.

"Mom, what are you talking about?" Amber asks—not knowing what Anita's referring to, but figuring that whatever it is, it can't be good.

"You know what I'm talking about," she says loudly.

At this, Amber starts looking around and notices all the people looking at them. "Mom," she hisses, "I don't know what you are talking about, but you need to calm down. People are staring."

"You took $40 out of my wallet, and now you're acting all innocent!" Anita is oblivious to the onlookers.

As anyone who has ever done it will tell you, parenting teenagers is hard. Talking to them about wrongdoing is even harder. If Anita has reason to believe that Amber has taken money from her, she absolutely needs to address it. But making a heated accusation in a public place is not the best way to work through this issue. How should she talk about her worrisome conclusion in a way that leads to dialogue?

STATE MY PATH

If Anita's goal is to have a healthy conversation about a tough topic (e.g., "I think you're stealing from me"), her only hope is to stay in dialogue—at least until she confirms or disproves her concerns. That holds true for anybody with any Crucial Conversation (e.g., "It feels like you micromanage me"; "I think you're using drugs"; "You threw me under the bus in the meeting"). That means that despite your worst suspicions, you shouldn't violate respect. In a similar vein, you shouldn't kill safety with threats and accusations.

So what should you do? Start with Heart. Think about what you *really* want and how dialogue can help you get it. And master your story—realize that you may be jumping to a hasty Victim, Villain, or Helpless Story. The best way to find out the true story is not to *act out* the worst story you can generate. That will lead to self-destructive silence and violence games. Think about other possible explanations long enough to temper your emotions so you can get to dialogue. Besides, if it turns out you're right about your initial impression, there will be plenty of time for confrontations later on.

Once you've worked on yourself to create the right conditions for dialogue, you can then draw upon five distinct skills that can help you talk about even the most sensitive topics. These five tools can be easily remembered with the acronym STATE. It stands for:

- **S**hare your facts.
- **T**ell your story.
- **A**sk for others' paths.
- **T**alk tentatively.
- **E**ncourage testing.

The first three skills describe *what* to do. The last two tell *how* to do it.

THE "WHAT" SKILLS

The best way to share your view is to follow the Path to Action model we learned in Chapter 5 from beginning to end—the same way you traveled it (Figure 8.1). Isn't it odd that we allow ourselves to move left to right along the path, but when we try to persuade others, we demand that they simply accept our feelings and stories without allowing them to do the same? When we're drunk on adrenaline, we lack either the wisdom or patience for reasoning. Since we're obsessing on our emotions and stories, we expect others to join us there. Starting with our ugly stories is the most controversial, least influential, and most insulting way we could begin.

Figure 8.1 Path to Action

Share Your Facts

So let's start on the left. The first step is to retrace your Path to Action to the source and find the facts—concrete evidence such as things you have seen, heard, or experienced directly. Anita can't find $40 in her wallet. That's a fact. She then told a story—the money isn't there because Amber stole it. Next, she felt betrayed and angry. Finally, she attacked Amber—"You little thief! I thought I could trust you!" The whole interaction was fast, predictable, and very ugly.

What if Anita took a different route—one that started with facts? What if she were able to suspend the ugly story she told herself (by intentionally thinking of alternative plausible stories) and then start her conversation with the facts? Wouldn't that be a safer way to go? Rather than planting a flag on the one story she generates, she assumes an attitude of curiosity—the fruit of humility. While she still has suspicions, she holds them tentatively for a moment while she explores other possibilities. How? By suspending the story and starting with the facts: the missing money.

Facts are the least controversial. Facts provide a safe beginning. By their very nature, facts are less controversial. For example, consider the statement, "Yesterday you arrived at work at 8:20 a.m." Little dispute there. Conclusions, on the other hand, are highly controversial. For example, "You were 20 minutes late" begins to include some story. It adds an assumption that you were expected to arrive at 8 a.m. Another option, "You can't be trusted," is hardly a fact. It's more like an insult, and it can certainly be disputed. Leaping from the 8:20 arrival to an assumption of tardiness to a story of unreliability moves us quickly from firm to questionable ground. Eventually we may want to share our conclusions, but we certainly don't want to open up with a controversy. Start with areas of least disagreement before moving to those with most.

Facts form the foundation for the conversation. Facts lay the groundwork for the conclusions that will come next. Facts become the starting point for the conversation and are less likely to spark offense. For example, which beginning is less offensive?

"Stop sexually harassing me!"

or

"When you talk to me, your eyes move up and down rather than look at my face. And sometimes you put your hand on my shoulder."

We want the other person to allow our meaning to be added to the shared pool. Before it is, it has to get a fair hearing. We're trying to help others see how a reasonable, rational, and decent person could end up with the story we're carrying. That's all. When we start with shocking or offensive conclusions ("Quit groping me with your eyes!" or "I think we should declare bankruptcy"), we encourage others to tell Villain Stories about us. Since we've given them no facts to support our conclusion, people are left to make up reasons we're saying these things. They're likely to believe we're either stupid or evil.

So if your goal is to help others see how a reasonable, rational, and decent person could think what you're thinking, start with your facts.

Take the time to sort out facts from conclusions. *Gathering the facts is the homework required for Crucial Conversations.*

Also, remember that you are sharing *your* facts. The skill here is to share your facts, not *the* facts. You are sharing what *you* have seen and heard. When you acknowledge that these are *your* facts, you make space for other facts—things the other person may have seen and heard. Sure, you have done your homework thoroughly in gathering the facts, but you don't pretend to have *all* the facts.

Tell Your Story

We're often far too eager to tell our stories (our judgments and conclusions). Sometimes just laying out the facts is enough to invite people into helping you make sense of them. For example, if your boss has failed to talk to HR about a raise for you three times in a row, it might be enough to point out the string of lapses without adding, "I think you're either a coward or a liar. Which is it?"

But by all means, if you do want to share your story, don't start with it. Your story (particularly if it has led to a rather harsh conclusion) could unnecessarily surprise or insult others. It could kill safety in one rash, ill-conceived sentence.

> **Brian:** *I'd like to talk to you about your leadership style. You micromanage me, and it's starting to drive me nuts.*

> **Fernando:** *What? I ask you if you're going to be done on time, and you lay into me with . . .*

If you start with your story (and in so doing, kill safety), you may never be able to actually get back to the facts. In order to talk about your stories, you need to lead the others involved down your Path to Action. Let them experience your path from the beginning to the end, and not from the end to—well, to wherever it takes you. Let others see your experience from your point of view—starting with your facts, followed by your story. This way, when you do talk about what you're starting to conclude, they'll understand why. First the facts, then the story—and make sure that as you explain your story, you tell it as a *possible* story, not as proven fact.

> **Brian:** (The facts.) *Since I started work here, you've asked to meet with me twice a day. That's more than with anyone else. You've also asked me to pass all my ideas by you before I include them in a project.*

> **Fernando:** *What's your point?*

> **Brian:** (The possible story.) *I'm not sure that you're intending to send this message, but I'm beginning to wonder if you don't trust me. Maybe you think that I'm not up to the job or that I'll get you into trouble. Is that what's going on?*

> **Fernando:** *Really, I was merely trying to give you a chance to get my input before you got too far down the path on a project. The last guy I worked with was constantly taking his project to near completion only to learn that he'd left out a key element. I'm trying to avoid surprises.*

Sharing your story can be tricky. You need to earn the right to share your story by starting with your facts. Even then, the other person can still become defensive when you move from facts to stories. After all, you're sharing potentially unflattering conclusions and judgments.

Why share your story in the first place? Because the facts alone are rarely worth mentioning. It's the facts plus the conclusion that call for a face-to-face discussion. In addition, if you simply mention the facts, the other person may not understand the severity of the implications. For example:

"I noticed that you had some of the new chip prototypes in your backpack."

"Yep, that's the beauty of these babies. They are tough enough to go anywhere."

"Those prototypes are proprietary."

"They ought to be! Our future depends on them."

"My understanding is that they're not supposed to go home."

"Of course not. That's how people steal them."

(Sounds like it's time for a conclusion.) *"I was wondering what the prototypes are doing in your backpack. It looks like you're taking them home. Is that what's going on here?"*

It takes confidence. It can be difficult to share negative conclusions and unattractive judgments (e.g., "I'm wondering if you're a thief"). It takes confidence to share such a potentially inflammatory story. However, if you've done your homework by thinking through the facts behind your story, you'll realize that you *are* drawing a reasonable, rational, and decent conclusion. One that deserves to be heard. And by starting with the facts, you've laid the groundwork. When you think through the facts and then lead with them, you're much more likely to have the confidence you need to add controversial and vitally important meaning to the shared pool.

Don't pile it on. Sometimes we lack the confidence to speak up, so we let problems simmer for a long time. Given the chance, we generate a whole arsenal of unflattering conclusions. For example, you're about to hold a Crucial Conversation with your child's second-grade teacher. The teacher wants to hold your daughter back a year. You want your daughter to advance right along with her age group. This is what's going on in your head:

> *I can't believe this! This teacher is straight out of college, and she wants to hold Jade back. I don't think she understands the stigma of being held back. Worse still, she's quoting the recommendation of the school psychologist. The guy's a real idiot. I've met him, and I wouldn't trust him with a common cold. I'm not going to let these two morons push me around.*

Which of these insulting conclusions or judgments should you share? Certainly not the entire menagerie of unflattering tales. In fact, you're going to need to work on this Villain Story before you have any hope of healthy dialogue. As you do, your story will begin to sound more like this (note the careful choice of terms—after all, it is your story, not the facts):

> *When I heard your recommendation, my initial reaction was to oppose your decision. But after thinking about it, I've realized I could be wrong. I don't really have any experience about what's best for Jade in this situation—only fears about the stigma of being held back. I know it's a complex issue. I'd like to talk about how both of us can objectively weigh this decision.*

Look for safety problems. As you share your story, watch for signs that safety is deteriorating. If people become defensive, step out of the conversation and rebuild safety by Contrasting. Here's how it works:

I know you care a great deal about my daughter, and I'm confident you're well trained. That's not my concern at all. I know you want to do what's best for Jade, and I do, too. My issue is that this is an ambiguous decision with huge implications for the rest of her life.

Be careful not to apologize for your views. Remember, the goal of Contrasting is not to water down your message, but to be sure that people don't hear more than you intend. Be confident enough to share what you really want to express.

Ask for Others' Paths

We mentioned that the key to sharing sensitive ideas is a blend of confidence and humility. We express our confidence by sharing our facts and stories clearly. We demonstrate our humility by then asking others to share their views—and meaning it.

So once you've shared your point of view, facts and stories alike, invite others to do the same. If your goal is to keep expanding the pool of meaning rather than to be right, to make the best decision rather than to get your way, then you'll willingly listen to other views. By being open to learning, you're demonstrating the curiosity that comes from true humility—a commitment to truth over ego.

For example, you might ask:

"How do you see it?"

"What's your perspective?"

"Can you help me understand?"

These open-ended questions encourage others to express their facts, stories, and feelings. When they do, carefully listen to what they have to say. Equally important, be willing to abandon or reshape your story as more information pours into the Pool of Shared Meaning. Remember, *what you really want* is to achieve valued results, not to gratify your ego by being right.

THE "HOW" SKILLS

Now that we've addressed the "what" skills in our STATE list of tools, we turn our attention to the two "how" skills.

Talk Tentatively

If you look back at the vignettes we've shared so far, you'll note that we were careful to describe both facts and stories in a tentative, or non-dogmatic, way. For example, "I'm beginning to conclude that . . ." or "I'm tempted to think . . ."

Talking tentatively simply means that we tell our story as a story rather than disguising it as a hard fact. "Perhaps you were unaware . . ." suggests that you're not absolutely certain of what the person knew. "In my opinion . . ." says you're sharing an opinion and no more.

When sharing a story, strike a blend between confidence and humility. Share in a way that expresses appropriate confidence in your conclusions while demonstrating that, if called for, you want your conclusions challenged. To do so:

Change	To
The fact is . . .	In my opinion . . .
Everyone knows . . .	I believe . . .
The only way to do this . . .	I am certain . . .
That's a stupid idea . . .	I don't think it will work . . .

Notice that the primary change from the left column to the right is not the degree of conviction expressed, but the level of honesty that this is simply your conviction. Even "The only way to do this . . ."

becomes more tentative when saying, "I am certain . . ." The first version sounds like a claim to absolute truth. The second acknowledges that this is simply your personal conviction.

"Talk tentatively" is not about softening the message; it's about strengthening it. Remember, your goal is to add meaning to the pool. And it won't make it into the pool unless the other person consents to it. If you attempt to disguise your conclusions as facts, the other person is likely to resist rather than consider them. Then nothing gets into the pool. One of the ironies of dialogue is that when there's a difference of opinions, the more convinced and forceful you act, the more resistant others become. Speaking in absolute and overstated terms does not increase your influence; it decreases it. The converse is also true—the more tentatively you speak, the more open people become to your opinions.

This raises an interesting question. Individuals have asked us if being tentative is the same as being manipulative. You're pretending to be uncertain about your opinion in order to help others consider it less defensively.

Our answer to this is an unequivocal *no*. If you're faking tentativeness, you're not in dialogue. The reason you should speak tentatively is because you aren't certain that your opinions represent absolute truth or that your understanding of the facts is complete and perfect. You should never pretend to be less confident than you are. But you should also not pretend to be more confident than your limited capacity allows. Your observations could be faulty. Your stories—well, they're only educated guesses.

Tentative, not wimpy. Some people are so worried about being too forceful or pushy that they err in the other direction. They wimp out by making still another Fool's Choice. They figure that the only safe way to share touchy data is to act as if it's not important: "I know this is probably not true . . ." or "Call me crazy, but . . ."

When you begin with a complete disclaimer and a tone that suggests you're consumed with doubt, you do the message a disservice. It's one thing to be humble and open. It's quite another to be clinically uncertain. Use language that says you're sharing an opinion, not language that says you're a nervous wreck.

A "Good" Story—the Goldilocks Test

To get a feel for how to best share your story, making sure you're not overstating or understating your convictions, consider the following examples:

Understated: *"This is probably stupid, but..."*

Overstated: *"How come you ripped us off?"*

Just right: *"It appears to me that you're taking this home for your own use. Is that right?"*

Understated: *"I'm ashamed to even mention this, but..."*

Overstated: *"Just when did you start using hard drugs?"*

Just right: *"It's leading me to conclude that you're starting to use drugs. Do you have another explanation that I'm missing here?"*

Understated: *"It's probably my fault, but..."*

Overstated: *"You wouldn't trust your own mother to make toast!"*

Just right: *"I'm starting to feel like you don't trust me. Is that what's going on here? If so, I'd like to know what I did to lose your trust."*

Understated: *"Maybe I'm just oversexed or something, but . . ."*

Overstated: *"If you don't find a way to pick up the frequency, I'm walking."*

Just right: *"I don't think you're intending this, but I'm beginning to feel rejected."*

Encourage Testing

When you ask others to share their paths, how you phrase your invitation makes a big difference. Not only should you invite others to talk, but you have to do so in a way that makes it clear that no matter how controversial their ideas might be, you want to hear them. Others need to feel safe sharing their observations and stories—particularly if they differ from yours. Otherwise, people don't speak up, and you can't test the accuracy and relevance of your views.

Safety becomes particularly important when you're having a Crucial Conversation with people who might move to silence. Some people make Fool's Choices in these circumstances. For example, some leaders refuse to weigh in on issues because they worry they'll shut down the dialogue. They worry that if they share their true opinions, others will clam up. So they choose between speaking their minds and hearing others out. But the *best* at dialogue don't choose. They do both. They understand that *the only limit to how strongly you can express your opinion is your willingness to be equally vigorous in encouraging others to challenge it.*

Invite opposing views. If you think others may be hesitant, make it clear that you want to hear their views—no matter how different. If their views disagree with yours, so much the better. If what they have to say is controversial or even touchy, respect them for finding the courage to express what they're thinking. If they have different facts or stories, you need to hear them to help complete the picture. Make sure they have the opportunity to share by actively inviting them to do so: "Does anyone see it differently?" "What am I missing here?" "I'd really like to hear the other side of this story."

Mean it. Sometimes people offer an invitation that sounds more like a threat than a legitimate call for opinions: "Well, that's how I see it. Nobody disagrees, do they?" Don't turn an invitation into a veiled threat. Invite people with both words and tone that say, "I really want to hear from you." For instance: "I know people have been reluctant to speak up about this, but I would really love to hear from everyone." Or "I know there are at least two sides to this story. Could we hear differing views now? What problems could this decision cause us?"

Play devil's advocate. Occasionally you can tell that others are not buying into your facts or story, but they're not speaking up either. You've sincerely invited them, even encouraged differing views, but nobody says anything. To help grease the skids, play devil's advocate. Model disagreeing by disagreeing with your own view: "Maybe I'm wrong here. What if the opposite is true? What if the reason sales have dropped is because our products truly are outdated. I know I've made the opposite case, but I really want to hear all the reasons my position could be dangerously wrong."

Encourage others until your motive becomes obvious. At times—particularly if you're in a position of authority—even being appropriately tentative doesn't prevent others from suspecting that you want them to simply agree with you or that you're inviting them into a trap. This may be the case when former bosses or authority figures have invited people to speak and then punished them for doing so.

This is where the skill of *encouraging testing* comes into play. As we said earlier, you can argue as vigorously as you want for your point of view, provided you are even more vigorous about encouraging others to disprove it. The real test of whether your motive is to win a debate or engage in real dialogue is the degree to which you encourage testing.

 CONFIDENCE AGAINST CANCER

The STATE skills help us share our meaning respectfully and effectively. Learn how one Crucial Conversations trainer used these skills to speak up and have a voice when deciding on treatment for a serious medical diagnosis. See her story in the video *Confidence Against Cancer* at crucialconversations.com.

Back to the Missing Money

To see how all the STATE skills fit together in a touchy conversation, let's return to the mystery of the missing $40. Anita reviews what happened as she and Amber are walking home from the store. This time, Anita will do a far better job of bringing up a delicate issue.

> **Anita:** (Shares facts.) *Amber, when I went to pay for the groceries just now, I was planning to use $40 that I thought I had in my wallet.*

> **Amber:** *Uh-huh.*

> **Anita:** (Shares facts.) *But when I opened my wallet, the money wasn't there. I thought it was strange, because I saw it there yesterday. Then I remembered you asking for some money last night to go out with your friends. I told you no. And you ended up going to a movie and dinner with them anyway.*

> **Amber:** *Uh-huh.*

Anita: (Tentatively tells story.) *Obviously one possibility is that you took the money.*

Amber: *You think I stole your money?*

Anita: (Asks for other's path.) *Honestly? I don't know what to think. All I know is what I just shared, and I hope you can see how I might at least have the question. Did you?*

Amber: *Um . . . well . . .*

Anita: (Contrasting.) *Amber, honey, I know you're a good kid, and I don't want to jump to hurtful conclusions. I also know people make mistakes. I did when I was your age. I want us to be able to talk about things, even hard things, honestly and openly, even when one of us has messed up.*

Amber: *I was planning to put it back. I wasn't trying to steal it. I didn't think you'd notice before I got my paycheck today.*

When this conversation actually did take place, it sounded exactly like the one portrayed above. The suspicious mother avoided nasty accusations and ugly stories, shared facts, and then tentatively shared a possible conclusion. As it turns out, her daughter had taken the money. They talked about it, and there were consequences for the theft. Amazingly, they also talked about the pressures that had led the daughter to take the money. Her mother learned more about what was going on in her daughter's life and was able to give some gentle coaching on how to handle some tough situations. She gained influence in her teenage daughter's life that day because of how she tackled a tough conversation.

WHEN STRONG BELIEF WEAKENS YOUR INFLUENCE

Now let's turn our attention to another communication challenge. This time you're not offering delicate feedback or iffy stories; you're merely going to step into an argument and advocate your point of view. It's the kind of thing you do all the time. You do it at home, you do it at work, you do it on social media, and yes, you've even been known to fire off an opinion or two while standing in line to vote.

Unfortunately, as stakes rise and others argue differing views—*and you just know in your heart of hearts that you're right and they're wrong*—you start pushing too hard. You simply have to win. There's too much at risk, and only you have the right ideas. Left to their own devices, others will mess things up. So when you care a great deal and are sure of your views, you don't merely speak—you try to force your opinions into the pool of meaning. You know, drown people in *your* truth. Quite naturally, others resist. You in turn push even harder.

We've watched this kind of thing happen all the time in our consulting work. For instance, seated around the table are a group of leaders who are starting to debate an important topic. First, someone hints that she's the only one with any real insight. Then someone else starts tossing out facts like so many poisonous darts. Another—it just so happens someone with critical information—retreats into silence. As emotions rise, words that were once carefully chosen and tentatively delivered are now spouted with an absolute certainty that is typically reserved for claims that are nailed to church doors or carved on stone tablets.

In the end, nobody is listening, everyone is committed to silence or violence, and the Pool of Shared Meaning remains parched and tainted. Nobody wins.

How Did We Get Like This?

It starts with a story. When we believe we're right and everyone else is wrong, we feel no need to expand the pool of meaning, because we *own* the pool. We also firmly believe it's our duty to fight for the truth that we're holding. It's the honorable thing to do. It's what people of character do.

Our stories that portray others as narrow-minded or dumb justify us in becoming controlling. "These poor people need saving," we tell ourselves. Soon we're modern-day heroes crusading against naïveté and tunnel vision.

We feel justified in using dirty tricks. Once we're convinced that it's our duty to fight for the truth, we start pulling out the big guns. We use debating tricks that we've picked up throughout the years. Chief among them is the ability to "stack the deck." We cite information that supports our ideas while hiding or discrediting anything that doesn't. Then we spice things up with exaggeration: "Everyone knows that this is the only way to go." When this doesn't work, we lace our language with inflammatory terms: "All right-thinking people would agree with me."

From there we employ any number of dirty tricks. We appeal to authority: "Well, that's what the boss thinks." We attack the person: "You're not so naïve as to actually believe that?" We draw hasty generalizations: "If it happened in our overseas operation, it'll happen here for sure." We attack a straw man: "Sure we can follow your plan—if we want to offend our top customers and lose the business."

And again, the harder we try and the more forceful and nasty our tactics, the greater the resistance we create, the worse the results, and the more battered our relationships.

How Do We Change?

The solution to employing excessive advocacy is actually rather simple—if you can just bring yourself to do it. When you find yourself just dying to convince others that your way is best, back off your current attack and think about what you really want for yourself, others, and the relationship. Then ask yourself, "What should I do right now to move toward what I really want?" When your adrenaline level gets below the 0.05 legal limit, you'll be able to use your STATE skills. In fact, your willingness to use STATE skills in sharing your message is a reliable indicator of your interest in dialogue. The harder it is for you to use them, the more likely your goal is to win rather than learn.

When you find yourself wanting to simply announce the truth rather than engage in dialogue, use the skills you've learned up to this point:

- **First, Learn to Look.** Watch for the moment when people start to resist you—perhaps they begin to raise their volume and/or overstate the facts behind their views in reaction to your tactics—or perhaps they retreat into silence. Turn your attention away from the topic (no matter how important) and onto yourself. Are you leaning forward? Are you speaking more loudly? Are you starting to try to win? Are you hammering on your keyboard as you furiously type a comment? Remember: *The more you care about an issue, the less likely you are to be on your best behavior.*

- **Second, check your intent.** What is your goal in the conversation? Do you want to be heard, understood, or validated? Maybe you want to change the other person's mind. You can't control or determine what another person will think at the end of a conversation, but you can influence it. As you consider what you really want from the conversation, ask yourself, "How would I behave if this is really what I want?"

For example, you and a coworker have been arguing about a recent high court ruling. No surprise there, as you and she are on opposite sides of the political spectrum. You feel passionately about this and want your coworker to change her views. So what is the best way to make that happen? It's probably not to yell, debate, disparage, or rebut. After all, when was the last time you changed your mind after someone unloaded an insulting rant on one of your opinions?

If you want to stand a chance at influencing people, you have to start by understanding them. So tone down your approach. Open yourself up to the belief that others might have something to say, and better still, they might even hold a piece of the puzzle—and then ask them for their views. Back off your harsh and conclusive language. But don't back off your belief. Hold to your belief; merely soften your approach.

My Crucial Conversation: Lori A.

Three years ago, my teenage daughter was diagnosed as bipolar. The manic highs and lows are incredibly frightening because they often turn violent, and the abyss of depression after [a violent episode] made me and my husband truly fear for our daughter's life.

With bipolar disorder, it takes a very long time to get the right combination of drugs to level the patient. Patients also have to be extremely consistent with their prescriptions. Of course, nonprescription drugs and alcohol are forbidden. During this difficult time, we had the police at our house to diffuse the violence. We watched helplessly as she used drugs and alcohol and cut herself. She stopped going to school. We had her hospitalized. We prayed a lot.

The good news is that I began using my Crucial Conversations skills during her manic highs and lows, and it worked! The Contrasting statement was extremely effective (and still is) in diffusing her anger and sadness. Later on, after she was level, the STATE My Path skills became a literal lifesaver. I noticed that if I was careful to remove my judgments when I shared my concerns and just state them factually, then encourage her to share her views, she could hear me much easier.

With the help of Crucial Conversations, I was able to maintain a relationship with my daughter during a time in her life when she was hard to reach. Since her diagnosis and treatment, she has truly turned her life around. She takes her medication, changed her friendships, goes to therapy, asks for support from her teachers when she is feeling stressed in school, volunteers with special-needs kids at church and, most importantly, talks to my husband and to me.

As we face more challenges ahead, I can and will continue to use these skills. In many ways, I believe you have helped us save her.

SUMMARY: STATE MY PATH

When you have a tough message to share, or when you're so convinced of your own rightness that you may push too hard, remember to STATE your path:

- **Share your facts.** Start with the least controversial, most persuasive elements from your Path to Action.
- **Tell your story.** Explain what you're beginning to conclude.
- **Ask for others' paths.** Encourage others to share both their facts and their stories.
- **Talk tentatively.** State your story as a story—don't disguise it as a fact.
- **Encourage testing.** Make it safe for others to express differing or even opposing views.

9

EXPLORE OTHERS' PATHS

How to Listen When Others Blow Up or Clam Up

"So, what risks do you all see in the current project plan?" Sanj asks. He looks at the team assembled around the table and sees blank face after blank face. A few people are looking down, diligently concentrating on their doodling. Others meet his eyes for a moment before looking away. No one says anything.

Sanj tries again: "I think we all know how important this project is. That's why we're here. If we are going to succeed, we have to be able to talk about the risks in the plan so that we can mitigate them. What are your concerns?"

More silence.

"OK, well then, great. That's just great," he says with obvious sarcasm. "I'll assume this is buttoned up. Good work, everyone. Now, let's go make it happen!"

As Sanj watches the team members gather their things and file out of the room, he looks down at the project plan again. A talented and experienced project manager, he has run several multimillion-dollar projects successfully, but never one quite like this. The project is already way behind, which is just one of the reasons the previous project manager was fired and Sanj was brought in. He's drafted a plan, but he knows he doesn't have the subject-matter expertise here to fill in all the gaps. That's why he has a team, for Pete's sake! But when he asks for people's input, he just gets blank stares. Nothing. Zip. Zilch. Nada. They just nod and tell him they like the plan. What else is he supposed to do?

Unfortunately, variations of this scenario are all too common. You know you need to have a Crucial Conversation with someone about a key project plan, or the trash piling up in front of your neighbor's door, or your son's new boyfriend and his colorful and slightly criminal history. Whatever the topic, you know the conversation will be crucial. So you prepare carefully. You find your good intent, master your stories, and carefully STATE your path. You genuinely want to hear the other person's point of view. And when you ask what the other person means, the person either looks at you with "deer in the headlights" eyes and says nothing or comes barreling at you with both guns blazing.

After the meeting, Sanj calls Tony, one of the team members, to get his take on things: "Hey, Tony, the group was pretty quiet in there. I am not sure whether everyone really agrees with the project plan or not. What do you think of the risks?"

"Oh, come on, Sanj," Tony replies. "Everyone knows this project is a train ride to Disaster Land. There is no way we get this out on time. And nobody is going to tell you to your face because you know what? You're *that* guy. The guy from corporate. The guy with a plan who's going to come in here on his white horse and save the day. Well, forget it, dude. This is a losing project, and the only question is who will still be on the ship when it sinks! And I'll tell you this . . . it's not going to be me. I am not taking the fall when this goes south. You are!"

"Wait a minute! That's not fair! You are on this team just as much as I am. I am not about to take the fall for this team's incompetence," Sanj jumps in loudly. "I'm the only one who cares about this project!"

HOW DO WE GET BACK TO DIALOGUE?

When others move to silence or violence, it can be tempting to join them there. After all, we've put in a lot of effort to open up the dialogue and invite them to share their meaning. When they don't share, or don't share well, our natural tendency is to get frustrated. All this talking is just wasted effort, right? "I do all the hard work, and they blow up or clam up." Our stories quickly spiral, and suddenly our motive shifts from wanting to understand their point of view to wanting to reinforce our own superiority.

So what should you do? After all, you aren't the one going to silence or violence. When others do damage to the pool of meaning by clamming up (refusing to speak their minds) or blowing up (communicating in a way that is abusive and insulting), is there something you can do to get them back to dialogue?

The answer is a resounding "It depends." If you want to let a sleeping dog lie (or, in this case, a potential train wreck go unattended), then say nothing. It's the other person who seems to have something to say but refuses to open up. It's the other person who's blown a cork. Run for cover. You can't take responsibility for someone else's thoughts and feelings. Right?

Then again, you'll never work through your differences until all parties freely add to the pool of meaning. That requires the people who are blowing up or clamming up to participate as well. And while it's true that you can't force others to dialogue, you can take steps to make it safer for them to do so. After all, that's why they've sought the security of silence or violence in the first place. They're afraid that dialogue will make them vulnerable. Somehow they believe that if they engage in real conversation with you, bad things will happen to them.

Sanj's team, for instance, is running scared. The team knows the project is in trouble. After all, the last project manager just got fired.

But people want to keep their jobs and have found that keeping their heads down is the best way to do that.

Restoring safety is your greatest hope for getting your relationships (and your teams, projects, and results) back on track.

EXPLORE OTHERS' PATHS

In Chapter 7, we recommended that whenever you notice safety is at risk, you should step out of the conversation and restore it. When you have offended others through a thoughtless act, apologize. Or if someone has misunderstood your intent, use Contrasting. Explain what you do and don't intend. Finally, if you're simply at odds, find a Mutual Purpose.

Now we'll add one more skill for helping restore safety: *Explore Others' Paths*. Since we've added a model of what's going on inside another person's head (the Path to Action), we now have a whole new tool for helping others feel safe. If we can find a way to let people know that it's OK to share their Path to Action—their facts and, yes, even their nasty stories and ugly feelings—then they'll be more likely to open up.

Exploring others' paths is a demonstration of our good intent, and that's why it's a powerful tool for creating safety. Thus far, we have shared our good intent by telling people what it is. This now is our chance to *show* them our good intent. If our intent truly is to listen, to understand, and to connect with them, how we act, not just what we say, will create safety.

But what does it take?

Start with Heart—Get Ready to Listen

Be sincere. To get others' facts and stories into the pool of meaning, we have to invite them to share what's on their minds. We'll look at how to do this in a minute. For now, let's highlight the point that when you do invite people to share their views, you must mean it. For example, consider the following incident: A patient is checking out of a health-care facility. The discharge clerk can tell that she is a bit uneasy, maybe even dissatisfied.

> **Clerk:** *Did everything go all right with the procedure?*
>
> **Patient:** *Mostly.* (If ever there was a hint that something was wrong, the term "mostly" has to be it.)
>
> **Clerk** (abruptly responds): *Good. Next!*

This is a classic case of pretending to be interested. It falls under the "How are you today?" category of inquiries. Meaning: "Please don't say anything of substance. I'm really just making small talk." When you ask people to open up, be prepared to listen.

Be curious. When you do want to hear from others (and you should, because it adds to the pool of meaning), the best way to get at the truth is by making it safe for them to express the stories that are moving them to either silence or violence. This means that at the very moment when most people become furious, we need to become curious. Rather than respond in kind, we need to wonder what's behind the ruckus. But how can we possibly act curious when others are either attacking us or heading for cover?

People who routinely seek to find out why others are feeling unsafe do so because they have learned that getting at the source of fear and discomfort is the best way to return to dialogue. They realize that the cure for silence or violence isn't to respond in kind, but to get at the underlying source. This calls for genuine curiosity—at a time when you're likely to be feeling frustrated or angry.

To illustrate what can happen as we exercise our curiosity, let's return to our nervous patient.

Clerk: *Did everything go all right with the procedure?*

Patient: *Mostly.*

Clerk: *It sounds like you had a problem of some kind. Is that right?*

Patient: *I'll say. It hurt quite a bit. And besides, isn't the doctor, like, uh, a little young to be practicing medicine?*

In this case, the patient is reluctant to speak up. Perhaps if she shares her honest opinion, she'll insult the doctor. Or maybe the loyal staff members will become offended. To deal with the problem, the clerk lets the patient know (as much with his tone as with his words) that it's safe to talk, and she opens up.

Stay curious. When people begin to share their volatile stories and feelings, we now face the risk of pulling out our own Victim, Villain, and Helpless Stories to help us explain why they're saying what they're saying. Unfortunately, since it's rarely fun to hear other people's critical stories, we begin to assign negative motives to them for telling the stories. For example:

Clerk: *Well aren't you picky! Read an article or two on the internet and now you think you know more about medicine than someone who graduated from medical school. Your doctor graduated top of her class. She's one of the best, you know.*

To avoid overreacting to others' stories, stay curious. A good way to distract your brain from spinning up stories of others' malicious motives is to give it a different problem to focus on. Like this one: "Why would a reasonable, rational, and decent person say this?" Then get busy trying to find an answer to this question. The tools below will help you do that. They'll help you actively retrace the other person's Path to Action until you see how it all fits together in a way you would find reasonable, rational, and decent. And in most cases, you end up seeing that under the circumstances, the individual in question drew a fairly reasonable conclusion.

Be patient. When others are acting out their feelings and opinions through silence or violence, it's a good bet they're starting to feel the effects of adrenaline. Even if we do our best to safely and effectively respond to the other person's verbal attack, we still have to face up to the fact that it's going to take a little while for him or her to settle down.

Say, for example, that a friend dumps out an ugly story and you treat it with respect and continue on with the conversation. Even if the two of you now share a similar view, it may seem like your friend is still pushing too hard. While it's natural to move quickly from one *thought* to the next, strong *emotions* take a while to subside. Thoughts are all electricity. Emotions add chemistry. Once the chemicals that fuel emotions are released, they hang around in the bloodstream for a time—in some cases, long after thoughts have changed. So be patient while the chemistry catches up with the electricity. Allow people time to explore their path and then wait for their emotions to catch up with the safety you've created.

Encourage Others to Retrace Their Path

Now that you've begun with an attitude of genuine curiosity, it's time to get to work. Your goal is to help others retrace their Path to Action. Recognize that we're joining the conversation at the *end* of their Path to Action. They've seen and heard things, told themselves a story or two, and generated a feeling (possibly a mix of fear, hurt, and anger or disappointment), and now they're starting to act out their story. That's where we come in. Now even though we may be hearing their first words, we're coming in somewhere near the end of their path. On the Path to Action model, we're seeing the action at the end of the path—as shown in Figure 9.1.

Figure 9.1   Path to Action

Every sentence has a history. Imagine a scenario where your favorite mystery show starts late because a football game runs long. As the game wraps up, the screen cross-fades from a trio of announcers to a starlet standing over a murder victim. Along the bottom of the screen are the discomforting words, "We now join this program already in progress."

You shake the remote in exasperation. You've missed the entire setup! For the rest of the program you end up guessing about key facts. What happened before you joined in?

Crucial conversations can be similarly mysterious and frustrating. When others are in either silence or violence, we're actually joining their Path to Action *already in progress*. Consequently, we've already missed the foundation of the story, and we're confused. If we're not careful, we can become defensive. After all, not only are we joining late, but we're also joining at a time when the other person is starting to act offensively.

Break the cycle. And then guess what happens? When we're on the receiving end of someone's accusations and cheap shots, we rarely think: "My, they have a lot of strong emotions right now. They must have told an interesting story. I wonder what it was and what led to it?" Instead, we match this unhealthy behavior. Our genetically shaped, eons-old defense mechanisms kick in, and we create our own hasty and unhelpful Path to Action.

People who know better stop this dangerous cycle by stepping out of the interaction and making it safe for the other person to talk about his or her Path to Action. They encourage him or her to move away from harsh feelings and knee-jerk reactions and toward the root cause. In essence, they retrace the other person's Path to Action together. At their encouragement, the other person moves from his or her emotions to what he or she concluded and then to what he or she observed.

When we help others retrace their path to its origins, not only do we help curb our reaction, but we also return to the place where the feelings can be resolved: their source—the facts and the story behind the emotion.

Inquiry Skills

When? So far we've suggested that when other people appear to have a story to tell and facts to share, it's our job to invite them to do so. Our cues are simple: Others are going to silence or violence. We can see that they're feeling upset, fearful, or angry. We can see that if we don't get at the *source* of their feelings, we'll end up suffering the *effects* of the feelings. These external reactions are our cues to do whatever it takes to help others retrace their Path to Action.

How? Whatever we do to invite the other person to share his or her path, our invitation must be sincere. As hard as it sounds, we must be genuine in the face of hostility, fear, or even abuse—which leads us to the next question.

What? What does it take to get others to share their path? In a word, it requires *listening*. To encourage people to move from acting on their feelings to talking about their conclusions and observations, we must listen in a way that makes it safe for them to share their intimate thoughts. They must believe that when they share their thoughts, they won't offend us or be punished for speaking frankly.

Ask, Mirror, Paraphrase, or Prime (AMPP)

To encourage others to share their paths, we'll use four power listening tools. We call the four skills *power* listening tools because they are best remembered with the acronym AMPP—*ask, mirror, paraphrase,* and *prime*. These tools work regardless of whether people are in silence or violence.

Ask to Get Things Rolling

The easiest and most straightforward way to encourage others to share their Path to Action is simply to invite them to express themselves. For example, often all it takes to break an impasse is to seek to understand others' views. When we show genuine interest, people feel less compelled to use silence or violence. Being willing to stop filling the pool with your meaning and invite the other person to talk about his or her view can go a long way toward getting to the source of the problem.

Common invitations include:

"What's going on?"

"I'd really like to hear your opinion on this."

"Please let me know if you see it differently."

"Don't worry about hurting my feelings. I really want to hear your thoughts."

Mirror to Confirm Feelings

If asking others to share their path doesn't open things up, mirroring can help build more safety. In mirroring, we take the portion of the other person's Path to Action we have access to and make it safe for him or her to discuss it. All we have so far are actions and some hints about the other person's emotions, so we start there.

We play the role of mirror by describing how the other person looks or acts. Although we may not understand others' stories or facts, we can see their actions and reflect them.

Mirroring is most useful when another person's tone of voice or gestures (hints about the emotions behind them) are inconsistent with his or her words. For example: "Don't worry. I'm fine." (But the person's look and tone suggest he's actually quite upset. He's frowning, looking around, and sort of kicking at the ground.)

Our response: "Really? From the way you're saying that, it doesn't sound like you are."

We explain that while the person may be saying one thing, his tone of voice or posture suggests something else. Mirroring magnifies safety because it demonstrates our genuine interest in and concern for others. We are paying attention! So much so, that we aren't just listening to *what* they are saying; we are noticing *how* they are saying it.

When reflecting your observations, take care to manage your tone of voice and delivery. It's not the fact that we're acknowledging others' emotions that creates safety. We create safety when our tone of voice says we're OK with them feeling the way they're feeling. If we do this well, they may conclude that rather than acting out their emotions, they can confidently talk them out with us instead.

So as we describe what we see, we have to do so calmly. If we act upset or as if we're not going to like what others say, we don't build safety. We confirm their suspicions that they need to remain silent.

Examples of mirroring include:

"You say you're OK, but the tone of your voice sounds upset."

"You seem angry with me."

"You look nervous about confronting him. Are you sure you're willing to do it?"

Ironically, when you sincerely acknowledge someone is angry with you, the person often begins to feel less angry. When you validate someone's nervousness, the person feels less need to be nervous. Mirroring can help others begin to talk out rather than act out their emotions.

Paraphrase to Acknowledge the Story

Asking and mirroring may help you get part of the other person's story out into the open. When you get a clue about *why* the person is feeling as he or she does, you can build additional safety by paraphrasing what you've heard. Be careful not to simply parrot back what was said. Instead, put the message in your own words—usually in an abbreviated form: "Let's see if I've got this right. You're worried because the previous project manager was fired. You're wondering if you or others on the project team might be at risk as well."

The key to paraphrasing, as with mirroring, is to remain calm and collected. Our goal is to make it safe, not to act horrified and suggest that the conversation is about to turn ugly. Stay focused on figuring out how a reasonable, rational, and decent person could have created this Path to Action. This task can help keep you from becoming angry or defensive. Simply rephrase what the person said, and do it in a way that suggests that it's OK, you're trying to understand, and it's safe for him or her to talk candidly.

Don't push too hard. Let's see where we are. We can tell that another person has more to share than he or she is currently sharing. He or she is going to silence or violence, and we want to know why. We want to get back to the source (the facts and story), where we can solve the problem. To encourage the person to share, we've tried three listening

198

tools. We've asked, mirrored, and paraphrased. The person is still upset, but isn't explaining his or her stories or facts.

Now what? At this point, we may want to back off. After a while, our attempts to make it safe for others can start feeling as if we're pestering or prying. If we push too hard, we violate both purpose and respect. Others may think our purpose is merely to extract what we want from them, and conclude that we don't care about them personally. So instead, we back off. Rather than trying to get to the source of the other person's emotions, we either gracefully exit or ask what he or she wants to see happen. Asking people what they want helps them engage their brains in a way that moves to problem solving and away from either attacking or avoiding. It also helps reveal what they think the cause of the problem is.

Prime When You're Getting Nowhere

On the other hand, there are times when you may conclude that others would like to open up but still don't feel safe. Or maybe they're still in violence, haven't come down from the adrenaline, and aren't explaining why they're angry. When this is the case, you might want to try priming. Prime when you believe that the other person still has something to share and might do so with a little more effort on your part.

The power-listening term "priming" comes from the expression "priming the pump." If you've ever worked an old-fashioned hand pump, you understand the metaphor. With a pump, you often have to pour some water into it to get it running. Then it works just fine. When it comes to power listening, sometimes you have to offer your best guess at what the other person is thinking or feeling before you can expect him or her to do the same. You have to pour some meaning into the pool before the other person will respond in kind.

A few years back, one of the authors was working with an executive team that had decided to add an afternoon shift to one of the company's work areas. The equipment wasn't being fully utilized, and the company couldn't afford to keep the area open without adding a three-to-midnight crew. This, of course, meant that the people currently working days would now have to rotate every two weeks to afternoons. It was a tortured but necessary choice.

As the execs held a meeting to announce the unpopular change, the existing employees went silent. They were obviously unhappy, but nobody would say anything. The operations manager was afraid that people would misinterpret the company's actions as nothing more than a grab for more money. In truth, the area was losing money, and the decision was made with the current employees in mind. With no second shift, there would be no jobs. He also knew that asking people to rotate shifts and to be away from loved ones during the afternoon and evening would cause horrible burdens.

As people sat silently fuming, the executive did his best to get them to talk so that they wouldn't walk away with unresolved feelings. He mirrored: "I can see you're upset—who wouldn't be? Is there anything we can do?" Nothing.

Finally, he primed. That is, he took his best guess at what they might be thinking, said it in a way that showed it was OK to talk about it, and then went on from there. He asked: "Are you thinking that the only reason we're doing this is to make money? That maybe we don't care about your personal lives?"

After a brief pause, someone answered: "Well, it sure looks like that. Do you have any idea how much trouble this is going to cause?" Then someone else chimed in, and the discussion was off and running.

Now this is not the kind of thing you would do unless nothing else has worked. You really want to hear from others, and you have a very strong idea of what they're probably thinking. Priming is an act of good faith, taking risks, becoming vulnerable, and building safety in hopes that others will share their meaning.

What If the Other Person Is Wrong?

Sometimes it feels dangerous to sincerely explore the views of someone whose path is wildly different from your own. He or she could be completely wrong, bigoted, or dangerous, and we're acting calm and collected. We feel like mounting a crusade, not asking a question!

To keep ourselves from feeling like sellouts while exploring others' paths—no matter how different or wrong they seem—remember we're trying to understand their point of view, not necessarily agree with it or support it. Understanding doesn't equate with agreement. Sensitivity doesn't equate to acquiescence. By taking steps to understand another person's Path to Action, we aren't promising that we'll accept their point of view. We are promising to listen.

There will be time later for us to share our path as well. For now, we're merely trying to get at what others think in order to understand why they're feeling the way they're feeling and doing what they're doing.

 HOW TO RESPECTFULLY DISAGREE ABOUT POLITICS

Having a Crucial Conversation can seem impossible with hot-button issues like politics. Coauthor Joseph Grenny has some tips for how to explore others' paths—even when you disagree—to turn a raging argument into a civil conversation. Watch the video *How to Respectfully Disagree About Politics* at crucialconversations.com.

SANJ'S TEAM—EXPLORING THE TEAM'S PATH

Let's put all the skills together in a single interaction by going back to Sanj and his team. The team has gathered for a morning huddle. Andrea is reporting on a critical milestone.

Andrea: *Despite the work we did, we still haven't completed the final cycle test. That will have to be done over the next week. I know this is later than expected, but I don't think anyone ever thought this was a realistic timeline to begin with.*

Sanj: *Wait. What? You signed up for this timeline. You agreed to it. If you didn't think it was realistic, you should have said something. Andrea, it's on you and your team to deliver what you have agreed to.*

Andrea: *We agreed to your timelines because there wasn't any other choice. Not because they were reasonable!*

Sanj's blood is starting to boil. He has always been a high performer, and he hates missing deadlines. If the team had been honest with him at the start, he could have flexed the schedule and maybe avoided this. He looks around the group. He can see the apprehension in their faces. It's clear this conversation isn't going well. Sanj is disappointed and irritated. Andrea is defensive and striking out. Sanj senses the crossroads he is at with the team right now. What happens next may well determine how they work together from here on and the ultimate success of the project.

He takes a pause and thinks, "What do I really want here?" Easy. He wants the project to succeed. Berating Andrea is not going to make that happen. Sanj knows he needs the team's help. The team members can see the land mines ahead that he's missing. He needs them to speak up with their concerns before it's too late.

Sanj: (Contrast to build safety.) *I don't want anyone to feel pressured to agree to a timeline he or she knows isn't realistic. That spells disaster for all of us. I want you all to feel like you can be open and candid about the risks ahead, without* *worrying that it will reflect poorly on you or the team. It won't. I don't want any deadline that we can't all win with.*

Tony: *That's easy for you to say. You're the star from corporate. Your job's not on the line.*

Sanj: (Ask.) *Can we talk about that for a minute? I've overheard several of you make comments about me being from corporate. I get the sense that you don't trust that I am on your side.*

(Silence)

Andrea (sounding nervous): *Of course not. Why wouldn't we trust you? I mean, you want this project to succeed, right?*

Sanj: (Mirror.) *The way you say that and how quiet everyone else is being make me wonder if you do trust me. In my experience, projects like this succeed when the whole team knows everyone has the same goal. Only then will we all feel safe being honest and candid about our concerns.* (Ask.) *I'd really like to know if there is something about me or the way I'm managing that's making that hard.*

(More silence)

Petr: *I think you're doing a great job, Sanj. We're happy you're here.*

Andrea: *Agreed. It isn't you. We're all just feeling a lot of pressure right now. I don't even want to think about what happens to all our jobs if this project tanks.*

Sanj: (Paraphrases.) *Oh, it sounds like maybe you think your jobs are at risk. Is that it?*

Andrea: *Um, yes? I mean, after what happened to our last project manager, shouldn't we be thinking that way?*

Sanj: (Prime.) *I can appreciate that concern. And yes, ultimately, all our jobs are tied to our performance. But I am wondering if there is something more going on here. Let me take a stab at something . . . I've heard a half-dozen references to me as "Singapore Sanj." People laugh when they say it, but now I wonder if there's some real concern that I only care about moving up in Singapore HQ and not making this project a real success. Are you worried that because I was put on this project by corporate that I am here evaluating you or something?*

(Team members glance nervously at one another.)

Andrea: *Well . . . um . . .*

Sanj: *Because if that is a concern, I want to address it right now. We all have a lot at stake with this project and . . .*

From here, the conversation goes to the real issues, the team discusses what's really going on, and both sides leave feeling more confident that they can speak up about concerns.

WHAT IF YOU DISAGREE? REMEMBER YOUR ABCS

Let's say you did your level best to make it safe for the other person to talk. After asking, mirroring, paraphrasing, and eventually priming, the other person opened up and shared his or her path. It's now your turn to talk. But what if you disagree? Some of the other person's facts are wrong, and his or her stories are completely fouled up. Well, at least they're a lot different from the story you've been telling. Now what?

Agree

As you watch families and work groups take part in heated debates, it's common to notice a rather intriguing phenomenon. Although the various parties you're observing are violently arguing, in truth, they're in *violent agreement*. They actually agree on every important point, but they're still fighting. They've found a way to turn subtle differences into a raging debate.

For example, last night your teenage son broke his curfew again. You and your spouse have spent the morning arguing about the infraction. The last time James came in late, you agreed to ground him, but today you're upset because it seems like your spouse is backpedaling by suggesting that James still be able to attend a football camp this week. Turns out it was just a misunderstanding. You and your spouse *agree* to the grounding—the central issue. You thought your spouse was reneging on the agreement when, in truth, you just hadn't actually resolved the date the grounding would start. You had to step back and listen to what you were both saying to realize that you weren't really disagreeing, but violently agreeing.

Most arguments consist of battles over the 5 to 10 percent of the facts and stories that people disagree over. And while it's true that people eventually need to work through differences, you shouldn't start there. Start with an area of agreement.

So here's the takeaway. If you completely agree with the other person's path, say so and move on. Agree when you agree. Don't turn an agreement into an argument.

Build

Of course, the reason most of us turn agreements into debates is because we disagree with a certain portion of what the other person has said. Never mind that it's a *minor* portion. If it's a point of disagreement, we'll jump all over it like the last piece of chocolate pie at the dessert buffet.

We do this because we're trained to look for minor errors from an early age. For instance, we learn in kindergarten that if you have the right answer, you're the teacher's pet. Being right is good. Of course, if others have the right answer, they get to be the pet. So being right first is even better. You learn to look for even the tiniest of errors in others' facts, thinking, or logic. Then you point out the errors. Being right at the expense of others is best.

By the time you finish your education, you have a virtual PhD in catching trivial differences and turning them into a major deal. So when another person offers up a suggestion (based on facts and stories), you're looking to disagree. And when you do find a minor difference, you turn this snack into a meal. Instead of remaining in healthy dialogue, you end up in violent agreement.

On the other hand, when you watch people who are skilled in dialogue, it becomes clear that they're not playing this everyday game of Trivial Pursuit—looking for trivial differences and then proclaiming them aloud. In fact, they're looking for points of agreement. As a result, they'll often start with the words "I agree." Then they talk about the part they agree with. At least, that's where they start.

Now when the other person has merely *left out an element* of the argument, skilled people will agree and then build. Rather than saying: "Wrong. You forgot to mention . . . ," they say: "Absolutely. In addition, I noticed that . . ."

If you agree with what has been said but the information is incomplete, build. Point out areas of agreement, and then add elements that were left out of the discussion.

Compare

Finally, if you do disagree, compare your path with the other person's. That is, rather than suggesting that the *other person* is wrong, suggest that you differ. He or she may, in fact, be wrong, but you don't know for sure until you hear both sides of the story. For now, you just know that the two of you differ. So instead of pronouncing "Wrong!," start with a tentative but candid opening. For example:

> *"I see things differently. Let me describe how."*

> *"I come at this from a different perspective."*

> *"My data stream is different from yours. Can I share it?"*

Then share your path using the STATE skills from Chapter 8. That is, begin by sharing your observations. Share them tentatively and invite others to test your ideas. After you've shared your path, invite the other person to help you compare it with his or her experience. Work together to explore and explain the differences.

In summary, to help remember these skills, think of your ABCs: *Agree* when you agree. *Build* when others leave out key pieces. *Compare* when you differ. Don't turn differences into debates that lead to unhealthy relationships and bad results.

SET EXPECTATIONS UP FRONT WHEN EXPLORING

When exploring others' paths, you are trying to create safety for people to share their meaning. But the pool expands only when their meaning is heard *and* when your meaning is heard. *Your* meaning needs to be in the pool as well. However, you will create more safety for others by helping them share their meaning first, before you dive into the pool with all your meaning. Start by listening, then sharing.

This can be hard, especially when we are concerned that others may want to share their meaning but don't want to hear ours. Uncle Carl is happy to spout off about his political views at the Thanksgiving dinner table. But the second someone voices a different opinion, he either rants or shuts down. How do you make sure you get a chance to be heard as well?

You can't force people to listen to you. Just because you listened to them doesn't necessarily mean they will listen to you. Still, most people will feel a sense of obligation to reciprocate. If you have sincerely listened and explored their path first, most people will be willing to listen in return. It can also help to set that expectation up front. For example, when Uncle Carl launches into his latest diatribe, take a moment to set some boundaries for the conversation. Let him know that you want to hear his perspective and ask him if he is willing to hear yours in return.

For example: "Uncle Carl, I can tell that you're really passionate about this, and I would sincerely like to explore and understand your point of view. I'm pretty sure it's different from mine, and it would be great to learn more about what you think. I'm committing to listening with an open mind. I wonder if, once I've done that, you'd be willing to listen to my point of view with an open mind. How about it?"

If Carl says no, then you can walk away from the conversation and feel OK about it. Nothing requires you to listen to his monologues. But chances are he'll agree to this reasonable request. Once he does, and it's your turn to share your perspective, don't be surprised if he needs a gentle reminder (or five of them!) of the commitment he made to listen.

My Crucial Conversation: Daryl K.

A few weeks ago, a friend I highly respect told me about *Crucial Conversations*. The notion of "Crucial Conversations" resonated with me because I'm in the midst of some challenging leadership issues, all of which involve potentially difficult conversations leading to important decisions. Anyway, the idea intrigued me enough that I went straight to the bookstore and bought the book. Once I began reading it, I couldn't put it down. I read it like a novel over that evening and the next morning, as every page seemed to offer help for the sticky situation I found myself in.

You see, I've been in the end stages of a major negotiation with a key partner. We want to jointly spin out a venture capital-funded company in Europe to further develop our technology. As we got closer to a deal over the last two months, the discussions started to decay, including heated phone calls and distrust on both sides. I was at a loss for how to effectively talk with the folks on the other side. Two weeks ago, we received a deal term sheet, so we had to either come together on an agreement or go our separate ways. If we went our separate ways, both sides knew it would end badly. So in desperation, last week I met with my negotiating counterparts to try to work through the impasses and strike a deal.

In preparing for the meeting, I reread the book, and it was like a light turning on for me. I went into the negotiations armed with a new communication approach. I literally scripted my arguments and had crib sheets on the dialogue process. I followed the basic process from the book, and it worked like a charm. There were many points where the dialogue started to decay, but each time I was able to restore it and move the discussion forward. One of the big things I had to do was fight my impulse to argue for my view and instead restore safety by simply exploring the other side's perspective. After a six-hour meeting, we emerged with the outline of a very good deal—for both parties.

The deal was finalized over the last two days. Negotiating the details of the final documents under tight time pressures, over the phone, and on two different continents was challenging and full of land mines. In fact, just yesterday at the moment of extreme tension, it seemed that the entire deal was coming unwound. I had to work the phones for four hours to rebuild dialogue between the parties so that we could get through the final pieces of the contract. Last night we were down to *one* word in the seventeen-page agreement. I wouldn't give in, and our partner's people tried to bully me. I had to step back—again—explore their views, and rebuild safety by finding a Mutual Purpose. We resolved the final piece very easily on a phone call at 5 a.m. in which I used the communication process to find common understanding between the parties.

I truly don't think that we would have struck the deal if a good friend had not recommended this powerful approach to communication.

SUMMARY: EXPLORE OTHERS' PATHS

To encourage the free flow of meaning and help others leave silence or violence behind, explore their Path to Action. Start with an attitude of curiosity and patience. This helps restore safety.

Then use four powerful listening skills to retrace the other person's Path to Action to its origins:

- **Ask.** Start by simply expressing interest in the other person's views.
- **Mirror.** Increase safety by respectfully acknowledging the emotions people appear to be feeling.
- **Paraphrase.** As others begin to share part of their story, restate what you've heard to show not just that you understand, but also that it's safe for others to share what they're thinking.
- **Prime.** If others continue to hold back, prime. Take your best guess at what they may be thinking and feeling.

As you begin to respond, remember:

- **Agree.** Agree when you share views.
- **Build.** If others leave something out, agree where you share views; then build.
- **Compare.** When you do differ significantly, don't suggest others are wrong. Compare your two views.

10

RETAKE YOUR PEN

*How to Be Resilient
When Hearing Tough Feedback*

One of the authors once gave a lengthy wedding toast to a happy couple. Every time he referred to the bride, he erroneously used the name
of the groom's ex-wife. He was feeling flush with confidence in his artful
delivery until after his fourth use of the wrong name. At that point a
cringing guest couldn't take it anymore and yelled out, "It's Bonnie, not
Becky!" Oops.

Critical feedback can be hard to hear. Some of the most Crucial
Conversations of all are when others tell you unpleasant things about
yourself. But there's a difference between getting feedback and being
feedsmacked. Most of us have been "feedsmacked" at some point in our
life. In the middle of a meeting, an innocent walk down the hallway, or a
performance review, someone delivers a verbal wallop that rocks your
psychological footing. And for some of us, life is never the same.

Take Carmen, for example. Carmen worked in a family business.
One day she asked her uncle, one of the founders, for some feedback.
He took off his glasses, locked his eyes on hers, and said, "You should

be more like your sister, Linda." Carmen recalls, "I was dumbfounded. Linda is petite, flirty, coy, and flattering to men. I am quite tall, independent, resourceful, and straightforward and work with men as equals." Then she adds, "Even though this happened decades ago, it still sticks in my mind."

We studied the stories of a few hundred people who had been feedsmacked at some point in their lives. Most told us of scars they carry to this day from these momentary encounters. When you read what they heard, it's easy to conclude that damage was unavoidable. Some were feedsmacked at work with statements like:

- *"You are an evil person. You are a thief. You are scum."*
- *"Quit being such a doormat for everyone who walks into your office. And please think about leaving—I need warriors, not wimps."*
- *"You are lazy and entitled."*
- *"You are venomous and poisonous."*
- *"You are kind of whiny."*
- *"You're lazy. I guess you just have no ambition or drive."*

Others reeled after an encounter at home:

- *"You're so desperate for someone to love that you're settling for your boyfriend."*
- *"For someone who is supposed to be a good communicator at work, you sure don't communicate well with me."*
- *"Who would hire you?"*
- *"You only want to have kids so you can have friends."*
- *"You're a worthless piece of @$#% and don't care about anyone but yourself."*

We were struck by how many could remember word for word what was said as though it were embroidered onto a mental sampler.

Sticks and stones may break bones, but these few words shattered self-confidence, hope, and, in some cases, life plans.

So what are we to do? Is it inevitable that our well-being can be demolished at any moment if the right person says the wrong thing?

FEEDBACK LESSONS FROM FELONS

We've spent much of our careers telling the world that the best way to help people receive and act on negative feedback is to improve how we deliver the message. In the previous chapters of this book, we've given you tools you can use to help others feel safe (Make It Safe) as you say the right things (CPR) in the right way (STATE My Path) for the right reasons (Start with Heart). And we stand by those ideas.

But we grossly underestimated how communication could be improved by improving people's ability to hear hard things, no matter how those messages are delivered. That is, until we met a hundred felons in downtown Salt Lake City, Utah (United States).

On the corner of 700 East and 100 South in Salt Lake City sits a three-story red brick Victorian mansion built in 1892. When it was completed, it boasted the city's first indoor plumbing. But today something far more innovative happens in it. It is now home to The Other Side Academy (TOSA). The inhabitants are 120 men and women who have been arrested an average of 25 times each. In most cases they've been running and gunning in crime, addiction, and homelessness for years or even decades. A woman we'll call Gloria, for example, lived under a bridge with her mother from the time she was five. When her mother introduced her to meth at age ten, she thought she found a superpower. When she applied to The Other Side Academy, she was facing charges for a brutal attack on her boyfriend. Another student named Jeffrey spent six years on the streets letting people do unspeakable things to him in order to stay high. A man we'll call Dominic embraced a promising start to a gang career by stabbing a homeless man. Students at TOSA have a lot of problems.

Most of the students stay for two to four years as an alternative to a new prison or jail sentence. During that time, they work hard to overcome a lifetime of self-destruction. There are no professionals at TOSA—no therapists, counselors, guards; nothing but a family of peers who have to find a way to be self-reliant. No one pays to come to TOSA. TOSA receives no tuition, insurance reimbursement, or funding from the government. Instead, the students run world-class businesses in order to generate income and to help them learn new habits of living and working with others.

When students arrive at TOSA, they often behave in ways that are impulsive, selfish, brooding, racist, lazy, defensive, and dishonest. Jail and prison aren't great prep schools for professional decorum. And no one got arrested for singing too loud in the church choir. If you've ever complained about the problem-people in your workplace, imagine what it would be like to try to run a business staffed entirely by TOSA students!

And yet for every year since their founding in 2015, TOSA businesses have been the top rated in their class. The Other Side Movers is the number one–rated moving company in the state. Figure 10.1 presents a customer review that's typical of the company's hundreds of five-star ratings.

The Other Side Builders has an impeccable reputation for integrity and quality. And if you read online reviews of The Other Side Thrift Boutique, you'd think people were describing a stay at a Four Seasons resort. How does this happen? How can deeply broken people come to work harmoniously together to accomplish results that would be the envy of the finest companies on the planet?

The answer: Games.

Every Tuesday and Friday night from 7 to 9 p.m., students gather for what TOSA calls "Games." TOSA leaders use the term to remind

  Berkeley R.   Aug 10, 2020

When I read all the amazing reviews of The Other Side Movers, I thought how on earth could a moving company have so many great reviews??!! Well, it's because they're AWESOME!

They charge an hourly rate and are SUPER fast, like running up and down the stairs fast. Not only are you getting a great price, you're getting super respectful, professional, conscientious guys who care about your stuff.

My foreman, Laef, went out of his way to show me the teeniest tiniest ding on a doorframe that I would have never noticed in a million years, but he felt compelled to show me because that's the kind of care they put into their work.

10 million stars, hire them if you get the chance!

Figure 10.1   A typical review of The Other Side Movers

students that, while like a sports game, TOSA Games can be intense and challenging, there are rules to keep them safe, they don't last forever, and you can move on when they're over. In Games, people sit in groups of 20 and give each other unvarnished feedback. The fundamental belief is that relentless exposure to truth is the best path to empathy, growth, and happiness.

Games can be loud. Vocabulary is sometimes raw. A single student can be the focus of a score of colleagues for 15 to 20 minutes without letup. Peers present you with evidence that you have acted dishonestly, manipulatively, lazily, selfishly, or arrogantly. There is little emphasis placed on diplomatic delivery of the message. Instead, peers focus on helping individuals learn to "take their game." Taking your game means, in essence, learning to listen nondefensively. Older students advise you to "just listen. Then put it all in a bag and take it to your pillow tonight. There you can decide what is gold and what is crap."

Now please understand, we are not telling you about Games to excuse you from your responsibility to deliver messages in respectful ways. Everything you've learned in this book calls for the opposite. The Other Side Academy has its own logic for why this unique population in this unique setting might benefit from this unique approach. But whether you agree or disagree with the reasoning, there is something striking we can learn from what happens to those who learn to not just participate, but thrive, in this kind of forum.

Unsurprisingly, newer students don't take their games very well. They withdraw, deny, or lash out against those who are telling them things they don't want to hear. But that changes quickly. They soon learn to let others say whatever they want to say, however they want to say it. They discover that they are the only sure source of their own sense of safety and worth. That discovery is liberating. They stop blaming the world for how they feel and become responsible for their own serenity.

Metaphorically speaking, they learn to retake their pen.

Think of your pen as the power to define your worth. When you hold your pen, you get to author the terms. Is your worth intrinsic to you? Is it about how you look? Is it contingent on how much you achieve, how many people admire you, or whether a certain person returns your love?

You're born with your pen firmly in your own grasp. Babies don't fret over others' opinions. We have no need for reassurance of something that seems beyond question. It doesn't matter to us that Grandma wishes we looked more like her, that Uncle would have liked us better if we had brown eyes, or that our older sister wanted us to be a girl. But that changes as we grow. As we become more aware of the emotions and judgments of those around us, a line gets crossed. We no longer look to others simply for help, information, or companionship—things they are qualified to offer us. Without realizing it, we hand them our pen.

Whoever holds your pen can compose the terms of your well-being. Some days you're in full possession of your pen. Some people like you. Some people don't. Some things go well. Some go poorly. But your personal security doesn't come from others' opinions of you; it comes from an innate sense of your enduring worth. Your psychological stock doesn't rise and fall based on whether someone laughs at your joke. You've got your pen.

But then one day a subtle shift happens without your awareness. You give a presentation that totally rocks. People nod when they should nod. They scribble notes at your every key insight. And at the end, a peer you've never spoken to tells you it was the best project pitch he's ever seen. It feels good. Really good. The committee meets and approves your proposal. That feels even better. Then your boss pulls you aside and says: "I've got big plans for you. Let's talk tomorrow." You look down and see your pen is now missing. You know it's circulating out there somewhere. But who cares? Life feels good.

A shift happens when we no longer look to others just for information. We begin to look to them for definition. We don't simply enjoy others' approval; we need it. From that moment we are fundamentally insecure. Those in possession of our pen now control our emotional well-being. As good as today feels, tomorrow is now pregnant with peril. To paraphrase the pastor Cornelius Lindsey, If you live by the compliment, you'll die by the criticism.

Sometimes we surrender our pens thoughtlessly. We don't notice the moment our center of gravity shifts. We lean too far forward and move from enjoying praise to needing it. Sometimes we do it out of a naïve hope that outside evidence will take better care of us than we can of ourselves. And other times it's just about a quick fix. We are unwilling to do the work required to steady ourselves, preferring to lean on approval instead. Then a Crucial Conversation or two remind us that this way of living makes us fundamentally unstable.

How you experience feedback has more to do with the location of your pen than the content of the message.

THE FEEDBACK PUZZLE

After watching TOSA students become masters of receiving feedback, we began to understand a puzzle in our own data. To help you appreciate what baffled us, read over this list of some of the "tough feedback" messages people reported getting. Next, rank-order them based on which you would guess was least to most hurtful to hear as reported by the subjects.

- *"You are venomous and poisonous."*
- *"You start conversations in the middle. You don't ask people if they have time; you just engage when it's convenient for you."*
- *"You are an evil person. You are a thief. You are scum."*
- *"When you lose your temper, it can make others feel less respected."*
- *"You need to take a deep look at yourself and find and eliminate your shortcomings."*

We've asked hundreds of people to perform this task. The most common sorting is:

1. *"You start conversations in the middle. You don't ask people if they have time; you just engage when it's convenient for you."*
2. *"When you lose your temper, it can make others feel less respected."*
3. *"You need to take a deep look at yourself and find and eliminate your shortcomings."*
4. *"You are venomous and poisonous."*
5. *"You are an evil person. You are a thief. You are scum."*

Notice that when you sort it this way, you make a tacit assumption. The sorting is based on the magnitude of the message. We assume that minor criticisms of easily changed behaviors would hurt much less than major judgments about deep character flaws. We have no doubt that being called "evil scum" would be deeply scarring, while being told

"You start conversations in the middle" would feel like a paper cut. It is this belief that distracts us from the work it takes to sever others' judgments from our worth.

Here is the actual ranking based on reports of our subjects of (a) how much the message hurt and (b) how long the hurt lasted:

1. *"You start conversations in the middle. You don't ask people if they have time; you just engage when it's convenient for you."*
1. *"When you lose your temper, it can make others feel less respected."*
1. *"You need to take a deep look at yourself and find and eliminate your shortcomings."*
1. *"You are venomous and poisonous."*
1. *"You are an evil person. You are a thief. You are scum."*

They were all equally, subjectively hurtful. Neither content nor delivery predicted the magnitude of the harm! Clearly something else was at play.

BACK TO THE OTHER SIDE ACADEMY

Our time at TOSA helped us see, once again, that how you feel about feedback is about who holds the pen, not what or how things are said. The very fact that we think the content or design of the feedback determines how we'll feel is our problem.

It's Friday night. The Game is on Marlin, a 55-year-old former junkie and prison alum who looks like a weathered seafarer. When at rest, his face defaults to grumpy. He has been at TOSA for three years. When he arrived, he was emotionally brittle. The slightest criticism or suggestion of disapproval sent him into an angry tirade. He was gamed relentlessly for being rude, self-absorbed, and defensive. But that was then.

He is now a foreman with The Other Side Builders. One of the newer students working under him brings him a full-throated game: "You're a control freak, Marlin. I'm not an idiot. I have construction experience. I know how to do things. But it doesn't matter if my way would work; it has to be your way! Do you get some kind of thrill out of keeping all of us under your thumb? Why can't you let me do it my way sometimes?"

Marlin takes it all in. He sits comfortably with his arms and legs relaxed. He looks calmly at the younger student as he pours out his complaint. As the student continues, Marlin's face becomes sad. When his colleague finishes, Marlin looks down, takes a breath, and says: "I didn't think about how this felt to you. You're right. That is what I do. I'll fix it."

Three years ago Marlin feared truth and craved approval. Today he craves truth and fears approval. He has learned to keep approval at a healthy distance—to treat it as information, not affirmation. How did that happen?

TWO PARTS OF THE PEN

He learned to retake his pen.

Let's elaborate a bit on the idea of the pen. Feedback only hurts when we believe it threatens one or both of our most fundamental psychological needs: safety (perceived physical, social, or material security) and worth (a sense of self-respect, self-regard, or self-confidence).

Let's broaden the definition of the pen as the power to define what we need to secure both of these needs.

First, let's focus on the issue of safety. Many TOSA students grew up in conditions of perpetual insecurity. As a result, they carry a belief that their security is perpetually at risk, and, more importantly, that they are incapable of securing it. While your upbringing may have been different from theirs, many of us had experiences growing up that make us wary in some circumstances. As a result, we come into some conversations feeling an unnecessary amount of apprehension.

As we grow to adulthood and gain greater resources to care for ourselves, we fail to update our assumptions about our safety. And those assumptions control our lives. When our boss, our life partner, our neighbor, or a passenger on a subway starts to criticize us, we react emotionally far out of proportion to the real risk. Why? Because we've equated approval with safety and disapproval with danger. And we've failed to update the equation as our capacity to take responsibility for our safety has increased.

When we become adults, the pen is ours. We are responsible for and capable of caring for ourselves. Admittedly, there are times when feedback does include financial threats ("I'm going to fire you"), relational threats ("I'm going to leave you"), or even physical threats ("I'm going to hit you"). In these instances, some level of fear is the right response. But our analysis of the 445 episodes people reported in our study showed that immediate threats are a rare exception. In most cases, it is our defensive, combative, or resentful response to feedback that puts us at risk more than the feedback itself. And one reason we become so defensive is that we underestimate our capacity to protect ourselves. You don't get angry when you're confident. You get angry when you're scared.

Now let's talk about worth. Let's start with two assumptions:

1. That learning truth is an absolute good. The more truth you know, the better you can navigate life.
2. That others' feedback is either pure truth, pure falsehood, or some mixture of the two. Usually it's some mixture.

The sensible response to feedback would be to do what TOSA students do: Put it in a bag, sort out what's true, and discard the rest. But we don't. Instead, whether it's true, false, or a combination, we react to it indiscriminately with hurt, shame, fear, or anger. Why? Because we live with an undercurrent of worry that we aren't worthy. It is our fear that we're inadequate, unlovable, or worthless that makes the opinions of others so threatening. When others hold our pens, we live with a constant gnawing fear of their disapproval. Their feedback is no longer an indictment of our behavior; it is an audit of our worth.

When we surrender our pen, we simultaneously abdicate responsibility for defining the terms of our own worthiness. We stop generating feelings of worth and start looking for them. And that search perpetuates our feelings of insecurity.

Do we really live in a world so brittle that a single verbal stone can bring it crashing down? Not until we lose control of our pen.

THE FEEDBACK CURE

TOSA students become masters at receiving feedback. It's not uncommon to hear older students complain that "it's been too long since I've gotten a hard game. I don't want others to stop helping me grow." Four tools help them progress from feeling defined by feedback to being beneficiaries of it. These tools redirect them inside rather than outside to secure their safety and worth.

The tools form the acronym CURE.

1. **Collect yourself.** Breathing deeply and slowly reminds you that you are safe. It signals that you don't need to be preparing for physical defense. Being mindful of your feelings helps, too. Do your best to name them as you feel them. Naming them helps you put a little bit of daylight between you and the emotions. Are you hurt, scared, embarrassed, ashamed? If you can think about what you're feeling, you gain more power over the feeling. Also, identifying, examining, and critiquing the stories that led to your feelings can help (see Chapter 5). Some students collect themselves by consciously connecting

with soothing truths, for example, by repeating an affirmation like, "This can't hurt me. I'm safe" or "If I made a mistake, it doesn't mean I am a mistake." Marlin retook his pen and authored the terms of his own worth as well: "I have infinite, intrinsic, and eternal worth. Neither my past nor others' opinions define me. My worth is about my potential and my choices." Connecting with these ideas during Games anchors him. Some with beliefs in a higher power find prayer helpful in connecting with reassurance of their worth as well.

2. **Understand.** Be curious. Ask questions and ask for examples. And then just listen. As we learned in the previous chapter, curiosity can inoculate you against defensiveness. Focusing on understanding helps interrupt our tendency toward personalizing. It's hard to beat yourself up when you're busy solving a puzzle. The best "curiosity puzzle" is answering the question "Why would a reasonable, rational, decent person say what he or she is saying?" Detach yourself from what is being said as though it is being said about a third person. That will help you bypass the need to evaluate what you're hearing. Simply act like a good reporter trying to understand the story.

3. **Recover.** It's sometimes best at this point to ask for a time-out. Feelings of control bring feelings of safety. And you regain a sense of control when you exercise your right to respond when you're truly ready. Explain that you want some time to reflect and you'll respond when you have a chance to do so. Like TOSA students, separate the tasks of collecting and sorting. Put it all in a bag and sort it out later. Give yourself permission to feel and recover from the experience before doing any evaluation of what you heard. At TOSA, students sometimes simply say, "I will take a look at that." They don't agree. They don't disagree. They simply promise to look sincerely at what they were told on their own timeline. They

put it in the pool of meaning and let it marinate until they are in full possession of their pens. You can end a challenging episode by simply saying: "It's important to me that I get this right. I need some time. And I'll get back to you to let you know where I come out." Then use whatever practices work for you to reconnect with a sense of safety and worth.

4. **Engage.** Examine what you were told. If you've done a good job reestablishing feelings of safety and worth, you'll look for truth rather than defensively poking holes in the feedback. Sift through the bag/pool of meaning. Even if it's 95 percent junk and 5 percent gold, look for the gold. There is almost always at least a kernel of truth in what people are telling you. Scour the message until you find it. Then, if appropriate, reengage with the person who shared the feedback and acknowledge what you heard, what you accept, and what you commit to do. At times, this may mean sharing your view of things. If you're doing so with no covert need for approval, you won't need to be defensive or combative.

Today Marlin carries himself with an easy confidence. He is reunited with parents and siblings with whom he had been at war for 30 years. Over 3 years he participated in 300 Games. That's a lot of feedback. But what Marlin came to learn is that how he responded to the feedback was more important than the feedback itself. He came to see Games he took badly as a reminder that he had inner work to do. As he learned to be the steward of his own safety and worth, he cultivated a peace that has changed everything.

It turns out that the misery we feel when "feedsmacked" is a symptom of a much deeper problem. Those who acknowledge and address this deeper issue don't just get better at these Crucial Conversations; they become better equipped for all of life's vicissitudes.

SUMMARY: RETAKE YOUR PEN

When you find yourself reacting to hard feedback, remind yourself that your reaction is largely within your control. "Retake your pen" by taking steps to secure your safety and affirm your worth. Then use four skills to manage how you address the information others share:

1. **Collect yourself.** Breathe deeply, name your emotions, and present yourself with soothing truths that establish your safety and worth.

2. **Understand.** Be curious. Ask questions and ask for examples. And then just listen. Detach yourself from what is being said as though it is being said about a third person.

3. **Recover.** Take a time-out if needed to recover emotionally and process what you've heard.

4. **Engage.** Examine what you were told. Look for truth rather than defensively poking holes in the feedback. If appropriate, reengage with the person who shared the feedback and acknowledge what you heard, what you accept, and what you commit to do. If needed, share your view of things in a noncombative way.

PART III

HOW TO FINISH

The skills for wrapping up a Crucial Conversation are deceptively simple. Most people know they *should* do them. They just don't. And they pay dearly for their omission.

Don't make the mistake of glossing over them because they seem so obvious. They're a prime example of where "common sense" is not "common practice." Consistent application of these skills will help you prevent an enormous amount of avoidable cleanup that inevitably results from violated expectations and divergent memories.

The skills in Chapter 11, "Move to Action," will ensure you have clear expectations about how decisions will be made, and about who will do what by when following your Crucial Conversation.

11

MOVE TO ACTION

How to Turn Crucial Conversations into Action and Results

Up until this point we've suggested that getting more meaning into the pool helps with dialogue. In order to encourage this free flow of meaning, we've shared the skills we've learned by watching people who are gifted at dialogue. By now, if you've followed some or all of this advice, you're walking around with full pools. People who walk near you should hear the sloshing.

It's time we add two final skills. Having more meaning in the pool, even jointly owning it, doesn't guarantee that we all agree on what we're going to do with the meaning. We often fail to convert the ideas into action for two reasons:

- We have unclear expectations about how decisions will be made.
- We do a poor job of acting on the decisions we do make.

This can be dangerous. In fact, when people move from adding meaning to the pool to moving to action, it's a prime time for new challenges to arise.

DIALOGUE IS NOT DECISION-MAKING

The two riskiest times in Crucial Conversations tend to be at the beginning and at the end. The beginning is risky because you have to find a way to create safety, or else things go awry. The end is dicey because if you aren't careful about how you clarify the conclusion and decisions flowing from your Pool of Shared Meaning, you can run into violated expectations later on. This can happen in two ways.

How are decisions going to be made? First, people may not understand how decisions are going to be made. For example, Cara is miffed. Rene just forwarded a confirmation email to her for a three-day cruise; the email thanks him for the reservation and the $500 deposit he has paid to secure an upgrade to an outside suite.

A week ago, they had a Crucial Conversation about vacation plans. Both expressed their views and preferences respectfully and candidly. It wasn't easy, but at the end they decided a cruise suited both quite well. And yet now Cara is upset. Rene is bewildered; he thought Cara would be ecstatic.

Cara agreed *in principle* about a cruise. She didn't agree to this particular cruise. Rene thought that any cruise would be fine and made a decision on his own. Have fun on the cruise, Rene.

Are we ever going to decide? The second problem with decision-making occurs when no decision gets made. Crucial Conversations are tough. By the time we navigate successfully to the end of one, we are often so incredibly relieved that we made it through that we simply and quickly end with a heartfelt expression of gratitude: "Thanks. I am really glad we could have this conversation." We walk away feeling better because, hey, no one cried, and no one yelled. Chalk one up in the win column. But because we haven't clarified our understanding or solidified decisions, ideas slip away and dissipate, or people can't figure out what to do with them.

DECIDE HOW TO DECIDE

We can solve both these problems if, before making a decision, the people involved decide how to decide. Don't allow people to assume that dialogue is decision-making. Dialogue is a process for getting all relevant meaning into a shared pool. That process, of course, involves everyone. However, allowing—even encouraging—people to share their meaning doesn't mean they are then guaranteed to take part in making all the decisions. To avoid violated expectations, separate dialogue from decision-making. Make it clear how decisions will be made—who will be involved and why.

When the line of authority is clear. When you're in a position of authority, you decide which method of decision-making you'll use. Managers and parents, for example, decide how to decide. It's part of their responsibility as leaders. For instance, VPs don't ask hourly employees to decide on pricing changes or product lines. That's the leaders' job. Parents don't ask small children to pick their home security device or to set their own bedtime. That's the job of the parent. Of course, both leaders and parents turn more decisions over to their direct reports and children when they warrant the responsibility, but it's still the authority figure who decides what method of decision-making to employ. Deciding what decisions to turn over and when to do it is part of their stewardship.

When the line of authority isn't clear. When there is no clear line of authority, deciding how to decide can be quite difficult. For instance, consider a conversation you had with your daughter's schoolteacher. The teacher suggested you should hold your child back. You're not sure. But whose choice is this anyway? Who decides whose choice it is? Does everyone have a say, then a vote? Is it the school officials' responsibility, so they choose? Since parents have ultimate responsibility, should they consult with the appropriate experts and then decide? Is there even a clear answer to this tough question?

A case like this is hand-tooled for dialogue. All the participants need to get their meaning into the pool—including their opinions about who should make the final choice. That's part of the meaning you need to discuss. If you don't openly talk about who decides and why, and your opinions vary widely, you're likely to end up in a heated battle that can only be resolved in court. Handled poorly, that's exactly where these kinds of issues are resolved—*The Jones Family vs. Happy Valley School District.*

So what's a person to do? Talk openly about your child's abilities and interests *as well as* about how the final choice will be made. Don't mention lawyers or a lawsuit in your opening comments; this only reduces safety and sets up an adversarial climate. Your goal is to have an open, honest, and healthy discussion about a child, not to exert your influence, make threats, or somehow beat the educators. Listen to the opinions of the experts at hand and discuss how and why the experts should be involved. When decision-making authority is unclear, use your best dialogue skills to get meaning into the pool. Jointly decide how to decide.

The Four Methods of Decision-Making

When you're deciding how to decide, it helps to have a way of talking about the decision-making options available. There are four common ways of making decisions: command, consult, vote, and consensus. These four options represent increasing degrees of involvement. Increased involvement brings the benefit of increased commitment, but also the curse of decreased decision-making efficiency. So how do you decide who gets to decide? Savvy people choose whichever of these four methods of decision-making best suits their particular circumstances.

Command

Let's start with decisions that are made with no involvement whatsoever. This happens in one of three ways. Either we make autonomous decisions within our area of responsibility, or outside forces place demands on us (demands that leave us no wiggle room), or we turn decisions over to others and then follow their lead. In reality, *most* decisions in life are command decisions. We or others write the email, approve the purchase order, or design the presentation. The world would grind to a halt if involving others became a norm rather than an exception.

When you're the boss, you make a host of command decisions out of pure efficiency. And that is as it should be. A key to being an effective leader is knowing which decisions are worth slowing down to allow for some level of involvement in the form of consulting, voting, or consensus decision-making.

In the case of external forces, customers set prices, agencies mandate safety standards, and other governing bodies simply hand us demands. As much as employees like to think their bosses are sitting around making choices, for the most part they're simply passing on the demands of the circumstances. These are command decisions. With external command decisions, it's not our job to decide what to do. It's our job to decide how to make it work.

In the case of turning decisions over to others, we decide either that this is such a low-stakes issue that we don't care enough to take part or that we completely trust the ability of the delegate to make the right decision. More involvement adds nothing. In strong teams and great relationships, many decisions are made by turning the final choice over to someone we trust to make a good decision. We don't want to take the time ourselves and gladly turn the decision over to others.

Consult

Consulting is a process whereby decision makers invite others to influence them before they make their choice. You can consult with experts, a representative population, or even everyone who wants to offer an opinion. Consulting can be an efficient way of gaining ideas and support without bogging down the decision-making process. At least not too much. Wise leaders, parents, and even couples frequently make decisions in this way. They gather ideas, evaluate options, make a choice, and then inform the broader population.

Vote

Voting is best suited to situations where efficiency is the highest value—and you're selecting from a number of good options. Members of the team realize they may not get their first choice, but frankly they don't want to waste time talking the issue to death. They may discuss options for a while and then call for a vote. When facing several decent options, voting is a great time saver but should never be used when team members don't agree to support whatever decision is made. In these cases, consensus is required.

Consensus

This method can be both a great blessing and a frustrating curse. Consensus means you talk until everyone honestly agrees to one decision. This method can produce tremendous unity and high-quality decisions. If misapplied, it can also be a horrible waste of time. It should only be used with (1) high-stakes and complex issues or (2) issues where everyone absolutely must support the final choice.

Four Important Questions

When choosing among the four methods of decision-making, consider the following questions:

1. **Who cares?** Determine who genuinely wants to be involved in the decision along with those who will be affected. These are your candidates for involvement. Don't involve people who don't care.

2. **Who knows?** Identify who has the expertise you need to make the best decision. Encourage these people to take part. Try not to involve people who contribute no new information.

3. **Who must agree?** Think of those whose cooperation you might need in the form of authority or influence in any decisions you might make. It's better to involve these people than to surprise them and then suffer their open resistance.

4. **How many people is it worth involving?** Your goal should be to involve the fewest number of people while still considering the quality of the decision along with the support that people will give it. Ask: "Do we have enough people to make a good choice? Will others have to be involved to gain their commitment?"

Say It Out Loud

Once you have considered your options and decided how you'll decide, make sure you add this critical meaning to the pool. This may seem obvious, but we marvel at how often it's overlooked. For example, you have an important decision to make about key features for a new product. You want to gather a lot of meaning from various experts. You send out a meeting invite to "discuss new product features." The discussion is robust. You end the meeting with a pretty clear consensus among the gathered experts. Next, you review some market research, get feedback from the finance team, and do some limited customer testing. You take all this information in and then make a decision. Your decision.

This is a classic consult decision, and you feel great about it. Right up until you send the email to the initial group outlining the product features you decided on. Within minutes, your inbox is flooded with frustrated responses. The gist of these? "Why did you even bother to involve us if you were just going to do whatever you wanted anyway?"

What happened here? Well, you went into the initial meeting knowing this was going to be a consult decision. The group members came together, heard you ask for their input, and assumed this would be a consensus decision. This is a pretty understandable and frankly common misconception, especially when you're dealing with consult versus consensus decisions. It's also easy to avoid. Once you've decided how you'll decide, make sure everyone knows.

It can be as simple as saying: "Your input is critical here. And please be aware, this is a consult decision. I'll take your input along with that of others and make the decision."

Or "I'd like for this to be a consensus decision. But we need to make the decision today, and we only have an hour for this meeting. If we can come to consensus in that time frame, great. If not, I'll take all your input and make the final decision."

How about you? Here's a great exercise for teams or couples, particularly those that are frustrated about decision-making. Make a list of some of the important decisions being made in the team or relationship. Then discuss how each decision is currently made, and how each *should* be made—using the four important questions. After discussing each decision, decide how you'll make decisions in the future. A Crucial Conversation about your decision-making practices can resolve many frustrating issues.

MAKE ASSIGNMENTS—PUT DECISIONS INTO ACTION

Does every Crucial Conversation need to end with a decision? Not necessarily. If our goal in a conversation is to get unstuck and improve our results, then yes, most often we will need to end with a decision—what is going to be different because of this conversation? But sometimes we fill the pool with so much new meaning that we may not be ready to move to a decision at the end of the conversation. And that's OK. While a conversation doesn't necessarily need to end with a decision, it should always end with a commitment. It may be a commitment to change or take action. Or it may be a commitment, simple but sincere, to reflect on the new meaning that has been shared.

As you close your conversations with commitments, make sure you consider the following four elements (sometimes shortened to the acronym WWWF):

- **Who?**
- Does **what?**
- By **when?**
- How will you **follow** up?

Who?

To quote an English proverb, "Everybody's business is nobody's business." If you don't make an actual assignment to an actual person, there's a good chance that nothing will ever come of all the work you've gone through to make a decision.

When it's time to pass out assignments, remember, there is no "we." "We" when it comes to assignments actually means "not me." It's code. Even when individuals are not trying to duck an assignment, the term "we" can lead them to believe that others are taking on the responsibility.

Assign a name to every responsibility. This applies at home as well as at work. If you're divvying up household chores, be sure you've got a specific person to go with each chore. That is, if you assign two or three people to take on a task, appoint one of them the responsible party. Otherwise, any sense of responsibility will be lost in a flurry of finger-pointing later on.

Does What?

Be sure to spell out the exact deliverables you have in mind. The fuzzier the expectations, the higher the likelihood of disappointment. For example, the eccentric entrepreneur Howard Hughes once assigned a team of engineers to design and build the world's first steam-powered car. When sharing his dream of a vehicle that could run on heated water, he gave them virtually no direction.

After several years of intense labor, the engineers successfully produced the first prototype by running dozens of pipes through the car's body—thus solving the problem of where to put all the water required to run a steam-powered car. The vehicle was essentially a giant radiator.

When Hughes asked the engineers what would happen if the car got into a wreck, they nervously explained that the passengers would be boiled alive, much like lobsters in a pot. Hughes was so upset in what the crew came up with that he insisted they cut it up into pieces no larger than three inches. That was the end of the project.

Learn from Hughes. When you're first agreeing on an assignment, clarify up front the boundary conditions of what you want. For example, "I want a steam-powered car *that is at least as safe, cost effective, and feature-rich as petroleum-powered cars.*" Couples get into trouble in this area when one of the parties doesn't want to take the time to think carefully about the "deliverables" and then later on becomes upset because his or her unstated desires weren't met. Have you ever remodeled a room with a loved one? Then you know what we're talking about. Better to spend the time up front clarifying exactly what you want rather than waste resources and hurt feelings on the back end.

To help clarify deliverables, use Contrasting. If you've seen people misunderstand an assignment in the past, explain the common mistake as an example of what you *don't* want. If possible, point to physical examples. Rather than talk in the abstract, bring a prototype or sample. We learned this particular trick when hiring a set designer. The renowned designer talked in vague platitudes about what he would deliver, and it sounded great to us. "I'll make you a modern open office setting that can transform easily to a manufacturing look," he crooned while waving hands in suggestive gestures. Tens of thousands of dollars later he delivered something that looked more typical of *Star Trek* than Silicon Valley. We had to start over from scratch. From that day on, we've learned to point to pictures and talk about what we want and don't want: "*Don't* use furniture, colors, decorative items, or materials that would be unfamiliar to Fortune 500 employees," and "*Do* make it resemble the half-dozen typical looks in these pictures." The clearer the picture of the deliverable, the less likely you'll be unpleasantly surprised.

By When?

It's shocking how often people leave this element out of an assignment. Instead of giving a deadline, people simply point to the setting sun of "someday." With vague or unspoken deadlines, other urgencies come up, and the assignment finds its way to the bottom of the pile, where it is soon forgotten. Assignments without deadlines are far better at producing guilt than stimulating action. Goals without deadlines aren't goals; they're merely directions.

How Will You Follow Up?

Always agree on how often and by what method you'll follow up on the assignment. It could be a simple email confirming the completion of a project. It might be a full report in a team or family meeting. More often than not, it comes down to progress checks along the way.

It's actually fairly easy to build follow-up methods into the assignment. For example: "Call me on my cell phone when you finish your homework. Then you can go play with friends. OK?"

Or perhaps you'll prefer to rely on milestones: "Let me know when you've completed your library research. Then we'll sit down and look at the next steps." Milestones, of course, must be linked to a drop-dead date: "Let me know as soon you've completed the research component of this project. You've got until the last week in November, but if you finish earlier, give me a call."

Remember, if you want people to feel accountable, you must give them an opportunity to account. Build an expectation for follow-up into every assignment.

WWWF for When It's Personal

Ending a conversation by deciding who will do what by when and how you'll follow up seems fairly straightforward in a group setting or in our professional lives. Many organizations have defined meeting structures specifically designed to capture action items and record decisions. But for many of you reading this book, our guess is that you've been thinking about, and perhaps struggling with, a one-on-one or personal Crucial Conversation. Maybe it's with a boss, a peer, or a loved one. It's just as critical that you end those conversations with a plan for who will do what by when and how you will follow up. Otherwise you stand a good chance of having the same conversation over and over again. But how do you do it without sounding ridiculously bureaucratic?

Here are three tips for moving to action at the end of a personal Crucial Conversation:

First, summarize for understanding. It's always a good idea to recap the conversation to make sure both people are on the same page. It can be helpful to share why you're summarizing. For example: "Great. This has been a really helpful conversation, and it feels like we're in a really good place. I want to recap what we have talked about just to make sure I have it all right."

Second, make sure you have identified an action. What is going to change because of this conversation? Again, it can be helpful to share the why behind this: "I am so glad we have had this conversation. I feel like we're headed in a good direction. And I want to make sure I'm clear on what we each need to do differently going forward. In terms of my commitments, I'll ..."

Finally, you need to make a plan to follow up. No one's perfect, and there is a reasonably good chance that someone, maybe you, won't follow up perfectly on the commitments you've made. That's OK. That's being human, after all. But you want to have a plan in place to follow up so that you can catch things early and correct them sooner.

Following up with a direct report or your child is one thing. But how do you follow up with your boss, a senior leader, or a long-tenured peer? It can be helpful to think of this as more of a plan to check in rather than a plan to check up. For example: "I think this is great. Thanks for taking the time to really dig into this. I'll circle back next week for a quick check just to make sure that, after we have had some time to sit with this, everything still seems OK and on track for both of us."

DOCUMENT YOUR WORK

Once again, a proverb comes to mind: "One dull pencil is worth six sharp minds." Don't leave your hard work to memory. If you've gone to the effort to complete a Crucial Conversation, don't fritter away all the meaning you created by trusting your memories. Write down the details of conclusions, decisions, and assignments. Remember to record who does what by when. Revisit your notes at key times (usually the next meeting) and review assignments.

As you review what was supposed to be completed, hold people accountable. When someone fails to deliver on a promise, it's time for dialogue. Discuss the issue by using the STATE skills we covered in Chapter 8. When you hold people accountable, not only do you increase their motivation and ability to deliver on promises, but you create a culture of integrity.

SUMMARY: MOVE TO ACTION

Turn your successful Crucial Conversations into great decisions and united action by avoiding the two traps of violated expectations and inaction:

Decide How to Decide

- *Command.* Decisions are made without involving others.
- *Consult.* Input is gathered from the group and then a subset decides.
- *Vote.* An agreed-upon percentage swings the decision.
- *Consensus.* Everyone comes to an agreement and then supports the final decision.

Finish Clearly

- Determine *who* does *what* by *when.*
- Make the deliverables crystal clear.
- Set a *follow-up* time.
- Record the commitments and then follow up.
- Finally, hold people accountable to their promises.

12

YEAH, BUT

Advice for Tough Cases

As we meet with Crucial Conversations trainers around the world, they report that at the end of a class there is inevitably someone who raises a hand and says something in the form of "Yeah, but . . .". For example, "Yeah, but my boss would never respond like that!" or "Yeah, but my teenager could ignore a tsunami!" Another common one is "Yeah, but what if I'm not carrying my training manual with me when the crucial moment hits?" In short, people can think of a dozen reasons why the skills we've been talking about don't apply to the challenges they face.

In truth, the dialogue skills we've shared apply to just about any problem you can imagine. However, since some situations are more difficult than others, we've chosen a few tough cases with which to illustrate the robustness of what you now know. We'll take a moment to share a thought or two on each.

SEXUAL OR OTHER HARASSMENT

"Yeah, but what if someone isn't blatantly harassing me or anything, but I don't like the way I'm being treated? How can I bring it up without making enemies?"

The Danger Point

Someone is making comments or gestures that you find offensive. The person does it seldom enough and he or she is subtle enough that you're not sure if HR or your boss can even help. What can you do?

In these situations it's easy to think that the offender has all the power. It seems as if the rules of polite society make it so that others can behave inappropriately and you end up looking like you're over-reacting if you bring it up.

Generally speaking, a vast majority of these problems go away if they're privately, respectfully, and firmly discussed. Your biggest challenge will be the respect part. If you put up with this behavior for too long, you'll be inclined to tell a more and more potent Villain Story about the offender. This will jack up your emotions to the point that you'll go in with guns blazing—even if only through your body language.

The Solution

Tell the rest of the story. If you've tolerated the behavior for a long time before holding the conversation, own up to it. This may help you treat the individual like a reasonable, rational, and decent person—even if some of his or her behavior doesn't fit this description.

When you feel a measure of respect for the other person, you're ready to begin. After establishing a Mutual Purpose for the exchange, STATE your path. For example:

(Establish Mutual Purpose.) *"I'd like to talk about something that's getting in the way of my working with you.*

It's a tough issue to bring up, but I think it'll help us be better teammates if I do. Is that OK?"

(STATE My Path.) *"When I walk into your office, frequently your eyes move from my eyes downward. And when I sit next to you at a computer, sometimes you put your arm around the back of my chair. I don't know that you're aware you're doing these things, so I thought I'd bring them up because they send a message that makes me uncomfortable. How do you see it?"*

If you can be respectful and private but firm in this conversation, most problem behavior will stop. And remember, if the behavior is over the line and the person appears intentionally sexually aggressive, you should contact HR rather than attempt a private and dangerous conversation. Furthermore, if after a conversation like this, the behavior continues, involve HR to ensure your rights and safety are protected.

AN OVERLY SENSITIVE SPOUSE

"Yeah, but what do you do when your spouse is too sensitive? You try to give your spouse some constructive feedback, but he or she reacts so strongly that you end up going to silence."

The Danger Point

Often couples come to an unspoken agreement during the first year or so of their marriage that affects how they communicate for the rest of their marriage. Say one person is touchy and can't take feedback, or the other doesn't give it very well. In any case, they in effect agree to say nothing to each other. They live in silence. Problems have to be huge before they're discussed.

The Solution

This is generally a problem of not knowing how to STATE your path. When something bothers you, catch it early. Contrasting can also help: "I'm not trying to blow this out of proportion. I just want to deal with it before it gets out of hand." Share your facts: describe the specific behaviors you've observed: "When Jimmy leaves his room a mess, you use sarcasm to get his attention. You call him a 'pig' and then laugh as if you didn't mean it." Tentatively explain the consequences: "I don't think it's having the effect you want. He doesn't pick up on the hint, and I'm afraid that he's starting to resent you" (your story). Encourage testing: "Do you see it differently?"

Finally, Learn to Look for signs that safety is at risk, and Make It Safe. When you STATE things well and others become defensive, refuse to conclude that the issue is impossible to discuss. Think harder about your approach. Step out of the content, do what it takes to make sure your partner feels safe, and then try again to candidly STATE your view.

When spouses stop giving each other helpful feedback, they lose out on the help of a lifelong confidant and coach. They miss out on hundreds of opportunities to help each other communicate more effectively.

FAILED TRUST

> *"Yeah, but what if I just don't trust the person?* He missed an important deadline. Now I wonder how I could ever trust him again."

The Danger Point

People often assume that trust is something you have or don't have. Either you trust someone, or you don't. That puts too much pressure on trust. "What do you mean I can't stay out past midnight? Don't you trust me?" your teenage son inquires.

Trust doesn't have to be universally offered. In truth, it's usually offered in degrees and is very topic-specific. It also comes in two flavors—motive and ability. For example, you can trust me to administer CPR if needed; I'm motivated. But you can't trust me to do a good job; I know nothing about it.

The Solution

Deal with trust around the issue, not around the person.

When it comes to regaining trust in others, don't set the bar too high. Just try to trust them in the moment, not across all issues. You don't have to trust them in everything. To Make It Safe for yourself in the moment, bring up your concerns. Tentatively STATE what you see happening: "I get the sense that you're only sharing the good side of your plan. I need to hear the possible risks before I'm comfortable. Is that OK?" If they play games, call them on it. Also, don't use your mistrust as a club to punish people. If they've earned your mistrust in one area, don't let it bleed over into your overall perception of their character. If you tell yourself a Villain Story that exaggerates others' untrustworthiness, you'll act in ways that help them justify themselves in being even less worthy of your trust. You'll start up a self-defeating cycle and get more of what you don't want.

SHOWS NO INITIATIVE

> *"Yeah, but what if it's not something they're doing, but something they don't do?* Some members of my work team do what they're asked, but no more. If they run into a problem, they take one simple stab at fixing it. But if their efforts don't pay off, they quit."

The Danger Point

Most people are far more likely to talk about the presence of a bad behavior than the absence of a good one. When someone really messes up, leaders and parents alike are compelled to take action. However, when people simply fail to be excellent, it's hard to know what to say.

The Solution

Establish new and higher expectations. Don't deal with a specific instance; deal with the overall pattern. If you want someone to show more initiative, tell him or her. Give specific examples of when the person ran into a barrier and then backed off after a single try. Raise the bar and then make it crystal clear what you've done. Jointly brainstorm what the person could have done to be both more persistent and more creative in coming up with a solution.

For instance: "I asked you to finish up a task that absolutely had to be completed before I returned from a trip. You ran into a problem, tried to get in touch with me, and then simply left a message with my four-year-old. What could you have done to track me down on the road?" or "What would it have taken to create a backup strategy?"

Pay attention to ways you are compensating for someone's lack of initiative. Have you made yourself responsible for following up? If so, talk with that person about assuming this responsibility. Have you asked more than one person to take the same assignment so you can be sure it will get done? If so, talk to the person originally assigned about reporting progress to you early so you only need to put someone else on the job when there's a clear need for more resources.

Stop acting out your expectations that others won't take initiative. Instead, talk your expectations out and come to agreements that place the responsibility on the team members while giving you information early enough that you aren't left high and dry.

TOUCHY AND PERSONAL

"Yeah, but what if it's something hyperpersonal, like a hygiene problem? Or maybe someone's boring, and people avoid him or her. How could you ever talk about something personal and sensitive like that?"

The Danger Point

Most people avoid sensitive issues like the plague. Who can blame them? Unfortunately, when fear and misapplied compassion rule over honesty and courage, people can go for years without being given information that could be extremely helpful.

When people do speak up, they often leap from silence to violence. Jokes, nicknames, and other veiled attempts to sneak in vague feedback are both indirect and disrespectful. Also, the longer you go without saying anything, the greater the pain when you finally deliver the message.

The Solution

Use Contrasting. Explain that you don't want to hurt the person's feelings, but you do want to share something that could be helpful. Establish Mutual Purpose. Let the other person know your intentions are honorable. Also explain that you're reluctant to bring up the issue because of its personal nature, but since the problem is interfering with the person's effectiveness, you really must. Tentatively describe the problem. Don't play it up or pile it on. Describe the specific behaviors and then move to solutions.

Although these discussions are never easy, they certainly don't have to be offensive or insulting.

THERE'S MORE WHERE THAT CAME FROM

Crucial Conversations aren't just the big, anticipated, sometimes-dreaded conversations you carefully plan for and then hold with precision and grace. Most often, you stumble into them without warning, at any moment, and with nearly everyone. As you continue to practice your skills, you'll find you'll be better on your toes and more adept at navigating even the trickiest of situations. But we don't plan to abandon you here.

Rather, we have curated a vast library of these kinds of "Yeah, but" scenarios—situations when people find it challenging to use their skills. For example:

- How do you surface microaggressions or racism?
- How do you respond to false accusations?
- How do you tell the truth when it will come across as harsh, even brutal?
- How do you confront a liar?
- How do you speak truth to someone in power?
- How do you talk to someone you don't even respect?
- How do you speak up for your morals and values?

Over the years, we've offered tips, advice, and even scripts for just how to hold these Crucial Conversations in our weekly newsletter and blog, *Crucial Skills*. We welcome you to read along each week as we answer readers' real-life questions, and of course, we welcome your own. You can also search our database of over 1,000 previous responses to give you targeted advice when you need it most.

To find additional advice for these and other very Crucial Conversations, visit us at cruciallearning.com/blog.

13

PUTTING IT ALL TOGETHER

Tools for Preparing and Learning

If you read the previous pages in a short period of time, you probably feel like an anaconda that just swallowed a warthog. It's a lot to digest.

You may well be wondering at this point how you can possibly keep all these ideas straight—especially during something as unpredictable and fast moving as a Crucial Conversation.

This chapter will help with the daunting task of making dialogue tools and skills memorable and usable. First, we'll simplify things by sharing what we've heard from people who have changed their lives by using these skills. Second, we'll lay out a model that can help you visually organize the nine dialogue principles. Third, we'll walk you through an example of a Crucial Conversation where all the dialogue principles are applied.

TWO KEY PRINCIPLES

Over the years, we've learned a lot about how various readers turn these ideas into new habits. Some people make progress by picking one skill that they know will help them get to dialogue in a current Crucial Conversation. Simply taking action using a new tool is a great way to start. If doing so leads to better results, you're more likely to persist in using it until it becomes a habit.

Others focus less on skills and more on principles. For example, get started with increasing your capacity to get to dialogue by becoming more conscious of these two key principles.

Learn to Look. The first principle for positive change is Learn to Look. That is, people who improve their dialogue skills continually ask themselves whether they're in or out of dialogue. This alone makes a huge difference. Even people who can't remember or never learned the skills of STATE, or AMPP, or CURE, etc., are able to benefit from this material by simply asking if they or others are falling into silence or violence. They may not know exactly how to fix the specific problem they're facing, but they do know that if they're not in dialogue, it can't be good. And then they try something to get back to dialogue. As it turns out, trying something is better than doing nothing.

So remember to ask the following important question: "Are we playing games, or are we in dialogue?" It's a wonderful start.

Many people get additional help in learning to look from their friends. They study the book or go through training as families or teams. As they share concepts and ideas, they learn a common vocabulary. This shared way of talking about Crucial Conversations helps people change.

Perhaps the most common way that the language of dialogue finds itself into everyday conversation is with the statement, "I think we've moved away from dialogue." This simple reminder helps people catch themselves early on, before the damage is severe. As we've watched executive teams, work groups, and couples simply go public with the fact that they're starting to move toward silence or violence, others often recognize the problem and take corrective action: "You're right. I'm not telling you what needs to be said" or "I'm sorry. I have been trying to force my ideas on you."

Make It Safe. The second principle is Make It Safe. We've suggested that dialogue consists of the free flow of meaning and that the number one flow stopper is a lack of safety. When you notice that you and others have moved away from dialogue, do something to make it safer. Anything. We've suggested a few skills, but those are merely a handful of common practices. They're not all-inclusive. To no one's surprise, there are many things you can do to increase safety. If you simply realize that your challenge is to make it safer, 9 out of 10 times you'll intuitively do something that helps.

Sometimes you'll build safety by asking a question and showing interest in others' views. Sometimes an appropriate touch (with loved ones and family members—not at work where touching can equate with harassment) can communicate safety. Apologies, smiles, even a request for a brief "time-out" can help restore safety when things get dicey. The main idea is to Make It Safe. Do something to generate evidence that you care about others' interests and that you respect them. And remember, virtually every skill we've covered in this book, from Contrasting to priming, offers a tool for building safety.

These two levers form the basis for recognizing, building, and maintaining dialogue. When the concept of dialogue is introduced, these are the ideas most people can readily take in and apply to Crucial Conversations. Now let's move on to a discussion of the rest of the principles we've covered.

HOW TO PREPARE FOR A CRUCIAL CONVERSATION

Here's one last tool to help you turn these ideas into action. It's a powerful way of coaching yourself—or another person—through a Crucial Conversation. It can literally help you identify the precise place where you are getting stuck and the specific skill that can help you get unstuck.

Take a look at Table 13.1, "Coaching for Crucial Conversations." The first column in the table lists the nine dialogue principles we've shared. The second column summarizes the skills associated with each principle. The final column is the best place to start coaching yourself or others. This column includes a list of questions that will help you apply specific skills to your conversations.

Table 13.1 Coaching for Crucial Conversations

Principle	Skill	Crucial Question
1. Choose Your Topic (Chapter 3)	Unbundle, Choose, Simplify	What's the right topic to address to move toward what I really want?
	CPR (Content, Process/ Pattern, Relationship)	Is this a Content, Pattern/Process, or Relationship issue?
2. Start with Heart (Chapter 4)	Focus on what you really want	What am I acting like I really want? What do I really want? • For me? • For others? • For the relationship? What should I do right now to move toward what I really want?

Principle	Skill	Crucial Question
3. Master My Stories (Chapter 5)	Retrace my Path to Action	How am I behaving? What am I feeling? What story is creating those feelings?
	Separate Fact from story	Get back to the facts: What have I heard or seen that supports my story? Are there other facts that challenge my story?
	Watch for Three Clever Stories	Am I telling Victim, Villain, or Helpless Stories?
	Tell the Rest of the Story	What am I pretending not to know about my role in the problem?
		Why would a reasonable, rational, and decent person do this?
		What should I do right now to move toward what I really want?
4. Learn to Look (Chapter 6)	Look for when the conversation becomes crucial	Am I going to silence or violence? Are others?
	Look for safety problems	
	Look for your own Style Under Stress	
5. Make It Safe (Chapter 7)	Apologize when appropriate	Why is safety at risk? • Have I established Mutual Purpose? • Am I maintaining Mutual Respect?
	Contrast to fix or prevent misunderstanding	
	CRIB to get to Mutual Purpose	What will I do to rebuild safety?

(continued on next page)

Table 13.1 Coaching for Crucial Conversations (*continued*)

Principle	Skill	Crucial Question
6. STATE My Path (Chapter 8)	Share your facts Tell your story. Ask for others' paths Talk tentatively Encourage testing	Am I really open to others' views? Am I talking about the real issue? Am I confidently expressing my own views?
7. Explore Others' Paths (Chapter 9)	Ask Mirror Paraphrase Prime Agree Build Compare	Am I actively exploring others' views? Am I avoiding unnecessary disagreement?
8. Retake Your Pen (Chapter 10)	Collect Understand Recover Engage	What must I do to make myself feel safe? What must I do to affirm my own worth?
9. Move to Action (Chapter 11)	Decide how you'll decide Document decisions and follow up	How will we make decisions? Who will do what by when? How will we follow up?

LET'S SEE HOW IT ALL WORKS

Finally, we've included an extended case here to show how these principles might look when you find yourself in the middle of a Crucial Conversation. It outlines a tough discussion between you and your sister about dividing your mother's estate. The case is set up to illustrate where the principles apply and to briefly review each principle as it comes up in the conversation.

The conversation begins with you bringing up the subject of the family summerhouse. Your mother's funeral was a month ago, and now it's time to split up both money and keepsakes. You're not really looking forward to it.

The issue is made touchier by the fact that you feel that since you almost single-handedly cared for your mother during the last several years, you should be compensated. You don't think your sister will see things the same way.

Your Crucial Conversation

You: *We have to sell the summer cottage. We never use it, and we need the cash to pay for my expenses from taking care of Mom the past four years.*

Sister: *Please don't start with the guilt. I sent you money every month to help take care of Mom. If I didn't have to travel for my job, you know I would have wanted her at my house.*

You notice that emotions are already getting strong. You're getting defensive, and your sister seems to be angry. You're in a Crucial Conversation, and it's not starting well.

Choose Your Topic

You've got multiple topics competing for your attention: "How will you be reimbursed?" "How will you divide the remaining assets?" "Are there hurt feelings over caretaking?" "Is there mistrust or feelings of disrespect between you and your sister?" "Is grief over your mother's death mixing in?" And on and on. You can't make progress until you agree on a topic.

Since all the topics are important, you choose to show you care about your sister's feelings by letting her decide.

> **You:** (Priming.) *It sounds like we need to talk about some other things before we can get to the cottage issue. Do you think I've acted resentful about how you participated in Mom's care at the end? Is that what you'd like to discuss?*

Start with Heart

Pause and ask yourself what you really want. This is best done prior to getting together with your sister. That way when she becomes emotional, you've got a longer-term perspective that helps keep you on course.

Ultimately you want to be compensated fairly for the extra time and money you put in that your sister didn't. You also want a good relationship with your sister. You know she is grieving and may even be feeling guilty about not having been as involved at the end. You want to support her in working through those feelings. But you want to avoid making a Fool's Choice. So going into this topic, you ask yourself, "How can I ensure I'm treated fairly and still be supportive of my sister?"

Master My Stories

You recognize that you're telling yourself Victim and Villain Stories. You've felt resentful toward your sister because she has been involved less. But you also never shared those feelings with her. You turned her into a villain because that was easier than asking her to help out more. You "tell the rest of the story" by asking, "What am I pretending not to know about my role in the problem?" You can see clearly that you never spoke up about your needs and now blame her for not guessing that you wanted help.

You ask yourself, "Why would a reasonable, rational, and decent person have done what she did?" This helps you see that the fact that your mother lived one kilometer from you and your sister lived a two-hour plane flight away has a lot to do with how things turned out. Sure, your sister could have volunteered more, but there's more going on here than a lazy, uncaring sister.

You're now emotionally ready to open your mouth.

Learn to Look

Come into the conversation engaging at two levels: *content* and *process*. Pay attention to what your sister is saying (content). But also pay attention to signs that safety is at risk (process).

Your sister moved to violence with her response to your proposal about compensation. She became accusatory and raised her voice. Using Learn to Look, you recognize this as a sign that she feels unsafe.

Make It Safe

Contrast to help your sister understand your purpose. If people trust your *intent*, they feel safer dealing with touchy *content*.

> **You:** *I know we've both got a lot of feelings right now about a lot of things. We're grieving. And we have problems to solve. We have some history as siblings. I do want to work out the practical problems we have in a way that's fair to both of us. I don't want to suggest that these financial concerns have anything to do with how much you loved Mom. But I also want to be sure you know I love you and I'm here for you as*

you're grieving. I need you, too. Before we get to the expense stuff, what can I do to support you?

Sister: *Of course, I wish I could have been there more at the end. I feel awful about letting her down. And letting you down. But I also feel like you've used that against me.*

Retake Your Pen

It's tough to hear your sister's allegation that you've been intentionally guilt-tripping her. At first you feel defensive and want to lash out. But you take a breath. And you remind yourself that her opinion of you doesn't define you. You remind yourself that her feelings are hers, and you shift to a place of curiosity to understand her Path to Action. Why does she feel the way she does?

Explore Others' Paths

Priming, you ask: "It sounds like you've experienced things from me that make you think I have a grudge about how things went at the end. Is that right? What have I done that looked like that?"

As your sister continues to open up, you realize you have "acted out" rather than "talked out" some of your concerns. You apologize for that. You acknowledge that you have felt resentful at times, and that some of those feelings were unfair given how easy it was for you to help and how hard it was for her. Having resolved that issue, you move to the next topic.

STATE My Path

You still want to resolve your concerns about compensation.

You: *Can we talk about expenses now?*

You need to share your facts and conclusions with your sister in a way that will make her feel safe telling her story.

You: *It's just that I spent a lot of money taking care of Mom and did a lot of work caring for her instead of bringing in a nurse. I know you cared about Mom, too, but I honestly feel like I did more in the day-to-day caregiving than you did, and it only seems fair to use some of what she left us to repay a part of what I spent. Do you see it differently? I'd really like to hear.*

Sister: *OK, fine. Why don't you just send me a bill.*

It sounds as though your sister isn't really OK with this arrangement. You can tell her voice is tense and her tone is one of giving in, not of true agreement.

Explore Others' Paths

Since part of your objective is to maintain a good relationship with your sister, it's important that she add her meaning to the pool. Use the inquiry skills to actively explore her views.

You: (Mirror.) *The way you say that makes it sound like maybe that suggestion isn't OK with you.* (Ask.) *Is there something I'm missing?*

Sister: *No—if you feel like you deserve more than I do, you're probably right.*

You: (Prime.) *Do you think I'm being unfair? That I'm not acknowledging your contributions?*

Sister: *It's just that I know I wasn't around much in the last couple of years. I've had to travel a lot for work. But I still visited whenever I could, and I sent money every month to help contribute to Mom's care. I offered to help pay to bring in a nurse if you thought it was necessary. I didn't know you felt*

263

you had an unfair share of the responsibility, and it seems like your asking for more money is coming out of nowhere.

You: (Paraphrase.) *So you feel like you were doing everything you could to help out and are surprised that I feel like I should be compensated?*

Sister: *Well, yes.*

You understand your sister's story now and still disagree to a point. Use the ABC skills to explain how your view differs. You agree in part with how your sister sees things. Use building to emphasize what you agree with and to bring up what you differ on.

You: *You're right. You did a lot to help out, and I realize that it was expensive to visit as often as you did. I opted not to pay for professional home healthcare because Mom was more comfortable with me taking care of her, and I didn't mind that. I never told you I was doing that and never set an expectation that I might be treated differently in the estate division because of it. That's on me. I still think it's a reasonable request on my part to be recognized financially for helping avoid the home health nurse expense. But I didn't give you a chance to weigh in on that before making that decision. There were also some incidental expenses it doesn't sound like you were aware of. The new medication she was on during the last 18 months was twice as expensive as the old, and the insurance only covered a percentage of her hospital stays. It adds up.*

Sister: *So it's these expenses you're worried about covering? Could we go over these expenses to decide how to cover them?*

Move to Action

You want to create a definite plan for being reimbursed for these expenses, and you want it to be one you both agree on. Come to a consensus about what will happen, document *who* does *what* by *when*, and settle on a way to *follow up.*

> **You:** *I've kept a record of all the expenses that went over the amount both of us agreed to contribute. Can we sit down tomorrow to go over those and talk about what's fair to reimburse me for?*

> **Sister:** *OK. We'll talk about the estate and write up a plan for how to divide things up.*

Getting to Dialogue

You and your sister still have a lot to work through. But getting all your meaning into the pool, and encouraging your sister to add hers, got you to dialogue. With a free flow of meaning, your future discussions are likely to be more helpful and less painful than if you hadn't stepped up to this conversation and handled it well.

My Crucial Conversation: Afton P.

One summer my husband secured a coveted internship in Geneva, Switzerland, working for the United Nations. While we were there, I befriended the Geneva representative for a nongovernmental organization (NGO) for women. She was gearing up for the upcoming Subcommission on the Promotion and Protection of Human Rights.

Believing in the importance of this committee's work, I became involved in their efforts to seek UN support to prevent human rights abuses to children. The focus was on child abduction and safety, and specifically, the oppression of religious expression, child soldiers, and young girls being sold into sex slavery. These abhorrent practices were being largely ignored by officials of some countries.

As the committee got to work planning the report we would present to the subcommission, I became concerned about what was and wasn't being shared. It was strongly suggested by the committee chair of our NGO that we avoid mentioning specific country names where the grievances were taking place. As a 22-year-old student not steeped in politics, I asked, "Why not?" The committee said it had to take extreme caution not to offend certain country officials who "looked the other way" regarding these abuses for fear of damaging relationships.

I was in a predicament; I wanted to promote real change, but I believed our report would hold little weight if we just talked in general terms, and I was afraid of losing a powerful opportunity in this forum. I immediately thought about the book *Crucial Conversations* and was kicking myself for not having brought it with me—who knew I'd need it on my summer abroad in Switzerland? Thankfully, I remembered the basics, and I drew on its principles as I expressed my belief that it was possible to be both candid and respectful in presenting delicate information.

To my surprise, they invited me to rewrite the report. I was thrilled, but also terrified about the potential harm I could cause if I wasn't very careful in addressing people from many nations with diverse cultures. I spent almost every waking hour and several sleepless nights trying to carefully script an honest yet respectful portrayal of the issues by stating the facts and focusing on a mutual purpose—human rights for suffering children. The committee agreed my version was more forthright and showed appropriate sensitivity.

The surprises continued: Ten days before the presentation, the committee asked me to present the report to the subcommission! I was both shocked and honored. Although this brought my anxiety level to a new peak, I immediately agreed to do it, and I spent the next several days and sleepless nights preparing for the event.

When my turn finally came to deliver the report, I felt exhilarated and a little anxious. After I finished presenting, it appeared many in the audience were moved, and a few even had tears in their eyes. Others hurried over to ask me for a copy of my speech for networking and documenting purposes. As they approached, some were emotional, and many thanked me for raising the sensitive issues.

I learned many lessons through this experience, but one that stands out is the importance of realizing it is possible to be both candid and respectful with the right set of skills. Knowledge of Crucial Conversations skills helped me turn an intimidating experience into a memorable and meaningful opportunity to stand up for something I believed in.

CONCLUSION: IT'S NOT ABOUT COMMUNICATION. IT'S ABOUT RESULTS

Let's end where we started. We began this book by suggesting we got dragged somewhat unwillingly into the topic of communication. What we were most interested in was *not* writing a book on communication. Rather, we wanted to identify *crucial moments*—moments when people's actions disproportionately affect their organizations, their relationships, and their lives. Our research led us time and again to focus on moments when people need to step up to emotionally and politically risky conversations. That's why we came to call these moments *Crucial Conversations*. We found that time and again what stands between us and what we really want is *lag time*. The problem isn't that we have problems. The problem is the lag time between when we know we have them and when we find a way to effectively confront, discuss, and resolve them. If you reduce this lag time, everything gets better.

Our sole motivation in writing this book has been to help you improve the results you care about most. And our dearest hope as we conclude it is that you will do so. Take action. Identify a Crucial Conversation you could improve *now*. Use the tools in this last chapter to identify the principle or skill that will help you approach it in a more effective way than you ever have. Then give it a try.

One thing our research shows clearly is that you need not be perfect to make progress. You needn't worry if you make only stuttering progress. We promise you that if you persist and work at these ideas, you will see dramatic improvement in your relationships and results. These moments are truly crucial, and a little bit of change can lead to an enormous amount of progress.

NOTES

Chapter 1

1. Clifford Notarius and Howard Markman, *We Can Work It Out: Making Sense of Marital Conflict* (New York: G.P. Putnam's Sons, 1993), 20–22, 37–38.
2. Dean Ornish, *Love and Survival: The Healing Power of Intimacy* (New York: HarperCollins Publishers, 1998), 63.
3. Ornish, *Love and Survival: The Healing Power of Intimacy*, 54–56.

Chapter 2

1. Rodwin, B. A., Bilan, V. P., Merchant, N. B., Steffens, C. G., Grimshaw A. A., Bastian, L. A., and Gunderson, C. G., "Rate of Preventable Mortality in Hospitalized Patients: A Systematic Review and Meta-analysis," *J Gen Intern Med*. 2020 July, 35(7): 2099–2106. Epub 2020 Jan 21. https://pubmed.ncbi.nlm.nih .gov/31965525/.

INDEX

ABOUT THE AUTHORS

Joseph Grenny is an author, speaker, and social scientist for business performance. He has advised leaders on every major continent, from the boardrooms of Fortune 500 companies to the communities in Nairobi, Kenya. He has cofounded three not-for-profit organizations: Unitus Labs, The Other Side Academy, and The Other Side Village.

Kerry Patterson has coauthored four award-winning training programs and led multiple long-term change efforts in Fortune 500 organizations around the world. He is the recipient of the BYU Marriott School of Management Dyer Award for outstanding contribution in organizational behavior. Kerry completed doctoral work at Stanford University.

Ron McMillan has consulted with thousands of leaders around the world, ranging from first-level managers to Fortune 500 executives. Prior to cofounding Crucial Learning (formerly VitalSmarts), Ron cofounded the Covey Leadership Center, where he served as vice president of research and development.

Al Switzler is a renowned consultant who has directed training and management initiatives with leaders from Fortune 500 companies worldwide. He also served on the faculty of the Executive Development center at the University of Michigan.

Emily Gregory, MD is the vice president of development and delivery at Crucial Learning. She leads product and content development and works with leaders to create custom learning solutions for their organizations. Emily holds a master's in business administration from Brigham Young University and a doctorate in medicine from the University of Utah.

About Crucial Learning

Formerly VitalSmarts, Crucial Learning improves the world by helping people improve themselves. By combining social science research with innovative instructional design, we create flexible learning experiences that teach proven skills for solving life's most stubborn personal, interpersonal, and organizational problems. We offer courses in communication, performance, and leadership, focusing on behaviors that have a disproportionate impact on outcomes, called crucial skills. Our award-winning courses and accompanying bestselling books include *Crucial Conversations, Crucial Accountability, Influencer, The Power of Habit,* and *Getting Things Done*. Together they have helped millions achieve better relationships and results, and nearly half of the Forbes Global 2000 have drawn on these crucial skills to improve organizational health and performance.

www.CrucialLearning.com

Also from the Crucial Learning Author Team

"*If you read only one 'management' book this decade . . . I'd insist that it be* Crucial Accountability."

—Tom Peters, author of *In Search of Excellence*

"*At Zappos, one of our core values is to 'Embrace and Drive Change.' This book shows how adapting one's life or career for the better can be done in a new and powerful way.*"

—Tony Hsieh, Former CEO of Zappos.com, Inc.

"*Influencing human behavior is one of the most difficult challenges faced by leaders. This book provides powerful insight into how to make behavior change that will last.*"

— Sidney Taurel, Chairman Emeritus, Eli Lilly and Company

"*Sharp, provocative, and useful.*"

—Jim Collins, author of *Good to Great*

"*I am a devout, card-carrying GTD true believer. The entire approach has boosted not only my productivity but also my wider well-being. . . . GTD has taken hold around the world. This is a genuine movement.*"

—Daniel Pink, author of *Drive*

Resources for Book Readers

Ever read a book on buoyancy and then assumed you'd be able to swim? Trust us, it doesn't work. Just like swimming, Crucial Conversations skills aren't something you master by reading a book, they're something you practice over and over again. And we've made it a lot easier.

The following resources are used in the award-winning Crucial Conversations course. Now they are being offered free to book readers. Simply access the resources at **CrucialConversations.com** and you're ready to go!

Crucial Conversations Video Examples

Not sure how to approach a Crucial Conversation? You're not alone. Watch examples and see real-life case studies using the skills taught in the book.

Discover Your Style Under Stress

What do you do when talking turns tough? To find out, fill out the Style Under Stress assessment. It'll help you see how you typically respond to a Crucial Conversation.

Cue Yourself with the Crucial Conversations Model

Now that you've read the book, one of the greatest challenges you'll face is simply remembering what you learned. Download this visual reminder of your new skills.

Join the Crucial Skills Community

Did you find the "Yeah, But" chapter helpful? Subscribe to our weekly e-newsletter and ask your own tough "yeah, but." Our authors and experts answer a reader's question each week.

Authors' Discussion Questions

Use these relevant discussion questions to guide your next book club or reading group.

Find these resources and more at CrucialConversations.com.